KU-652-300

SCM PAPERBACKS
by William Barclay

THE MIND OF JESUS

CRUCIFIED AND CROWNED

A NEW PEOPLE'S LIFE OF JESUS

NEW TESTAMENT WORDS

THE MASTER'S MEN

PRAYERS FOR THE CHRISTIAN YEAR

EPILOGUES AND PRAYERS

LETTERS TO THE SEVEN CHURCHES

THE LORD'S SUPPER

WILLIAM BARCLAY

Prayers for
the Christian Year

SCM PRESS LTD
BLOOMSBURY STREET LONDON

334 01287 2

First published 1964
Second impression 1969
Third impression 1971

© *SCM Press Ltd 1964*

Printed in Great Britain by
Richard Clay (The Chaucer Press), Ltd.,
Bungay, Suffolk

CONTENTS

PREFACE

THE Book of Common Prayer is not so much the possession of a Church as it is the possession of all who worship God in the English language. Its influence has left its mark on the worship-language of almost every English-speaking Church. In it a certain kind of liturgy and a certain kind of language reached a perfection which was never to be equalled, let alone surpassed.

The last thing, therefore, that this book wishes to do is to rewrite or to modernize the Collects of the Book of Common Prayer. Still less does it wish to provide a substitute for them. To seek to do that would be to be guilty of an insensitiveness and an arrogance well-nigh unforgivable. What has been done in this book is this. The Collect for the day has been set down in italics; and then below it there is a prayer in modern language which has been suggested by the Collect, or which has grown out of the Collect, or in which the substance of the Collect has been expanded. The Collects have been used as starting-points for devotion and for meditation.

In doing this the aim has been to get the best of both worlds. The aim has been at one and the same time to keep and to conserve the beauty and the magnificence of the ancient language untouched and unspoiled, and to link with it the meaningfulness and the newness of modern English. It may be that the ancient and the modern make strange bedfellows; but it has for a long time now seemed to me that, if we would make worship relevant to the modern man, we must use the language of the modern man, not in its slang and in its colloquialism, but in its simplicity. Each

6

generation must offer its own best to God, without forgetting and without abandoning that which has gone before.

It is my own hope and my own prayer that the prayers of this book may be found useful both for personal devotion and for public worship. Certainly for myself the use of the ancient Collects and the meditation upon them has been throughout the past year a moving and valuable exercise in devotion.

WILLIAM BARCLAY

The University of Glasgow,
Easter 1964

Almighty God, give us grace that we may cast away the works of darkness, and put upon us the armour of light, now in the time of this mortal life, in which thy Son Jesus Christ came to visit us in great humility; that in the last day, when he shall come again in his glorious Majesty to judge both the quick and the dead, we may rise to the life immortal, through him who liveth and reigneth with thee and the Holy Ghost, now and ever. Amen.

Epistle: Romans 13.8-14   *Gospel:* Matthew 21.1-13

O God, our Father, we thank you that you sent your Son Jesus Christ into this world to be our Saviour and our Lord.

We thank you that he took our body and our flesh and blood upon himself, and so showed us that this body of ours is fit to be your dwelling-place.

We thank you that he did our work, that he earned a living, that he served the public, and so showed us that even the smallest tasks are not beneath your majesty and can be done for you.

We thank you that he lived in an ordinary home, that he knew the problems of living together, that he experienced the rough and smooth of family life, and so showed us that any home, however humble, can be a place where in the ordinary routine of daily life we can make all life an act of worship to you.

Lord Jesus, come again to us this day.

> Come into our hearts, and so cleanse them, that we being pure in heart may see God, our Father.

> Come into our minds, and so enlighten and illumine them that we may know you who are the way, the truth, and the life.

> Touch our lips, that we may speak no word which would hurt another or grieve you.

> Touch our eyes, that they may never linger on any forbidden thing.

> Touch our hands, that they may become lovely with service to the needs of others.

> Come when we are sad, to comfort us; when we are tired, to refresh us; when we are lonely, to cheer us; when we are tempted, to strengthen us; when we are perplexed, to guide us; when we are happy, to make our joy doubly dear.

O God, our Father, help us so to live that, whenever your call comes for us, at morning, at midday or at evening, it may find us ready, our work completed, and our hearts at peace with you, so that we may enter at last with joy into your nearer presence and into life eternal; through Jesus Christ our Lord. Amen

The Second Sunday in Advent

Blessed Lord, who hast caused all holy Scriptures to be written for our learning: Grant that we may in such wise hear them, read, mark, learn, and inwardly digest them, that by patience, and comfort of thy holy Word, we may embrace, and ever hold fast the blessed hope of everlasting life, which thou hast given us in our Saviour Jesus Christ. Amen.

Epistle: Romans 15.4-13   *Gospel:* Luke 21.25-33

O God, this day we thank you for your Book.
> For those who wrote it, for those who lived close to you, so that you could speak to them and so give them a message for their day and for ours;
>> We thank you, O God.

> For those who translated it into our own languages, often at the cost of blood and sweat and agony and death, so that your word can speak to us in the tongue we know;
>> We thank you, O God.

> For scholars whose devoted and consecrated study and toil has opened the meaning of your Book to others;
>> We thank you, O God.

> For those who print it and publish it, and for the great Bible Societies whose work makes it possible for the poorest of people all over the world to possess your word;
>> We thank you, O God.

For its thrilling stories of high and gallant adventure;
For its poetry which lingers for ever in the memory of men;
For its teaching about how to live and how to act and how to speak;
For its record of the thoughts of men about you and about our blessed Lord;
For its comfort in sorrow, for its guidance in perplexity, for its hope in despair;
Above all else for its picture of Jesus:
> We thank you, O God.

Make us at all times
> Constant in reading it;
> Glad to listen to it;
> Eager to study it;
> Retentive to remember it;
> Resolute to obey it.

And so grant that in searching the Scriptures we may find life for ourselves and for others; through Jesus Christ our Lord. Amen.

The Third Sunday in Advent

O Lord Jesus Christ, who at thy first coming didst send thy messenger to prepare thy way before thee: Grant that the ministers and stewards of thy mysteries may likewise so prepare and make ready thy way, by turning the hearts of the disobedient to the wisdom of the just, that at thy second coming to judge the world we may be found an acceptable people in thy sight, who livest and reignest with the Father and the Holy Spirit, ever one God, world without end. Amen.

Epistle: I Corinthians 4.1-5   *Gospel:* Matthew 11.2-10

Lord Jesus, in your days in the body in Palestine you chose your men that you might send them out to do your work. We know that you are still looking for hands and voices and minds to use, and we ask you to bless those whom you are still sending out on your service.

> Bless the ministers of your Church in all its branches. Make them diligent in study, faithful in pastoral duty, wise in teaching, fearless and winsome in preaching, and ever clothed with your grace and love.

> Bless those who teach the young in schools, and colleges, and universities. Make them to think adventurously and to teach enthusiastically, that they may kindle and inspire young minds in the search for truth. Help them to be such that they may infect others with the contagion of the love of learning, dedicated to the service of mankind.

12

Bless those who heal and tend the sick, doctors, surgeons and nurses. Give them skill, gentleness and sympathy, so that, when it is possible to heal, they may do so, and, when it is not possible, they may bring help and comfort to those who enter into the valley of the shadow.

Bless fathers and mothers to whom you have committed the trust of a little child. Help them to build a home in which wise discipline and understanding walk hand in hand.

Bless those who do the world's work, and grant that whatever they do they may do for you, so that they may never offer less than their best, and so that they may be workmen who have no need to be ashamed.

So grant that all your servants, faithfully serving you and their fellow men, may prepare themselves and those amongst whom they work for your coming again.

This we ask for your love's sake. Amen.

O Lord, raise up (we pray thee) thy power, and come among us, and with great might succour us; that whereas, through our sins and wickedness, we are sore let and hindered in running the race that is set before us, thy bountiful grace and mercy may speedily help and deliver us; through the satisfaction of thy Son our Lord, to whom with thee and the Holy Ghost be honour and glory, world without end. Amen.

Epistle: Philippians 4.4-7   *Gospel:* John 1.19-28

Lord Jesus, send to us the power, the might, the grace, which we need so much to help us to overcome sin and to conquer our temptations.

> The purity of heart which will shut the door of our minds to every evil thought;
> The strength of will which will make us able to defy all temptations;
> The love of men which will banish for ever all bitterness, and which will make us to serve as you served, and to forgive as you forgave:
>> Grant us these things.

> The fidelity on which others can utterly rely;
> The diligence which will never offer less than its best;
> The will to work which hates all lazy idleness:
>> Grant us these things.

> The power of decision which will deliver us from all procrastination;

14

The perseverance which will refuse to leave anything half done;

The courage to face the tasks we fear and do not want to do:

Grant us these things.

Grant that we may neither be too much lost in regrets for the past or dreams for the future, but grant that we may do with our might that which lies to our hand, so that we may fight the good fight, and finish the race, and keep the faith, and so at the end receive the crown of righteousness which you will award to those who have been faithful.

This we ask for your love's sake. Amen.

Christmas-Day and the Sunday after Christmas-Day

Almighty God, who hast given us thy only-begotten Son to take our nature upon him, and as at this time to be born of a pure Virgin: Grant that we being regenerate, and made thy children by adoption and grace, may daily be renewed by thy Holy Spirit; through the same our Lord Jesus Christ, who liveth and reigneth with thee and the same Spirit, ever one God, world without end. Amen.

Christmas-Day:

Epistle: Hebrews 1.1-12   *Gospel:* John 1.1-14

The Sunday after Christmas-Day:

Epistle: Galatians 4.1-7   *Gospel:* Matthew 1.18-25

O God, our Father, we remember at this Christmas time how the eternal Word became flesh and dwelt among us.

We thank you that Jesus took our human body upon him, so that we can never again dare to despise or neglect or misuse the body, since you made it your dwelling-place.

We thank you that Jesus did a day's work like any working-man, that he knew the problem of living together in a family, that he knew the frustration and irritation of serving the public, that he had to earn a living, and to face all the wearing routine of everyday work and life and living, and so clothed each common task with glory.

16

We thank you that he shared in all happy social occasions, that he was at home at weddings and at dinners and at festivals in the homes of simple ordinary people like ourselves. Grant that we may ever remember that in his unseen risen presence he is a guest in every home.

We thank you that he knew what friendship means, that he had his own circle of men whom he wanted to be with him, that he knew too what it means to be let down, to suffer from disloyalty and from the failure of love.

We thank you that he too had to bear unfair criticism, prejudiced opposition, malicious and deliberate misunderstanding.

We thank you that whatever happens to us, he has been there before, and that, because he himself has gone through things, he is able to help those who are going through them.

Help us never to forget that he knows life, because he lived life, and that he is with us at all times to enable us to live victoriously.

This we ask for your love's sake. Amen.

Saint Stephen's Day

Grant, O Lord, that in all our sufferings here upon earth for the testimony of thy truth, we may stedfastly look up to heaven, and by faith behold the glory that shall be revealed; and, being filled with the Holy Ghost, may learn to love and bless our persecutors by the example of thy first Martyr Saint Stephen, who prayed for his murderers to thee, O blessed Jesus, who standest at the right hand of God to succour all those that suffer for thee, our only Mediator and Advocate. Amen.

Lesson: Acts 7.55-60   *Gospel:* Matthew 23.34-49

O God, our Father, help us ever to see eternity beyond time. When loyalty to Jesus brings suffering and trial,

> Help us to remember,
>> That we walk in the footsteps of the saints and the martyrs;
>> That our reward in heaven is great, for you will be in no man's debt;
>> That beyond the cross there waits the crown;
>> That through it all we have the promise that he is with us always to the end of the world and beyond.

Give us grace, O God, to love and to pray even for those who hurt and wrong us.

18

Grant, O God of love,

> That injury may not awaken in us the desire for
> revenge;
>
> That injustice may not embitter us;
>
> That unfair criticism and even slander may not
> enrage us.

But grant that,

> We may meet hatred with love,
>
> And injury with forgiveness.

To that end make us at all times to look to our Blessed
Lord at your right hand and to remember,

> that there is nothing which we must suffer
> that he has not already suffered;
>
> that because he has gone through it,
> he can help others who are going through it.

Lord Jesus, help us to bear your cross that we may share
your crown. This we ask for your love's sake. Amen

Saint Stephen's Day is 26th December.

Saint John the Evangelist's Day

Merciful Lord, we beseech thee to cast thy bright beams of light upon thy Church, that it being enlightened by the doctrine of thy blessed Apostle and Evangelist Saint John may so walk in the light of thy truth, that it may at length attain to the light of everlasting life; through Jesus Christ our Lord. Amen.

Epistle: 1 John 1.1-10   *Gospel:* John 21.19-25

O God, our Father, give light to your whole Church and give light to each one of us.

Give us light that we may believe aright.
>So grant
>>That our beliefs may be right, certain, and true;
>>That no heresy and no false doctrine may disturb or destroy the faith;
>>That no self-will may blind us to the truth, making us wilfully refuse to see the things we ought to see.

Give us light that we may walk aright.
>So grant
>>That the light of truth may show us where we ought to go;
>>That the knowledge of the truth may guide us in all our decisions;
>>That we may ever walk with him who is the Way, the Truth, and the Life.

20

Grant that we may seek the truth aright.
So grant
> That we may seek the truth in the Gospel and the Letters of your Apostle John and in the whole Bible;
>
> That we may never be deaf to the voice of conscience or to the promptings of the Holy Spirit;
>
> That we may turn to you for guidance so that we may be guided where we cannot see.

Grant that we may reach the light of everlasting life.
So grant
> That guided by your light we may reach the light that never fades;
>
> That illumined by your truth we may reach the truth which is complete;
>
> That in the end we may see light in your light and know even as also we are known.

This we ask through Jesus Christ our Lord. Amen.

Saint John the Evangelist's Day is 27th December.

The Innocents' Day

O Almighty God, who out of the mouths of babes and sucklings hast ordained strength, and madest infants to glorify thee by their deaths: Mortify and kill all vices in us, and so strengthen us by thy grace, that by the innocency of our lives, and constancy of our faith even unto death, we may glorify thy holy Name; through Jesus Christ our Lord. Amen.

Lesson: Revelation 14.1-5   *Gospel:* Matthew 2.13-18

O God, our Father, this day we remember the little children who suffered by the cruelty of men in the days when Jesus, our blessed Lord, was born a child into this world.

This day we ask you to give us a childlike heart.

Give us,
> A child's innocence,
>> that we may be numbered with the pure in heart;
>
> A child's wonder,
>> that the loveliness of the world
>>> may be to us for ever new;
>
> A child's forgiveness,
>> that we may forget injustice and unfairness,
>>> as a child forgets;
>
> A child's obedience,
>> that as a child obeys a father,
>>> we may obey you;
>
> A child's trust,
>> that as a child trusts his parents for everything,
>> we may commit our lives in trust to you.

22

This day we ask you to give us a faithful heart.

Give us a heart
    So loyal,
        that we will never be ashamed to show,
            whose we are and whom we serve;
    So true to you,
        that we will remain true,
            even if we have to stand alone;
    So faithful to you,
        that no temptation and no seduction
            may ever lure us from your path.

And, if our fidelity should cost us something, make us glad for the opportunity to show how much we love you; through Jesus Christ our Lord. Amen.

The Innocents' Day is 28th December.

The Circumcision of Christ

Almighty God, who madest thy blessed Son to be circumcised, and obedient to the law for man: Grant us the true Circumcision of the Spirit; that, our hearts, and all our members, being mortified from all worldly and carnal lusts, we may in all things obey thy blessed will; through the same thy Son Jesus Christ our Lord. Amen.

Epistle: Romans 4.8-14   *Gospel:* Luke 2.15-21

O God, our Father, help us to express our religion, not in outward rituals and ceremonies and conventions, but in the inner devotion of our hearts, and in the true and ungrudging service of you and of our fellow men.

Make us to remember that no pious obedience to conventional acts can ever be a substitute for the love which expresses itself in sympathy and in practical help.

Make us to realize that consistent attendance at the services of your Church, diligent study of your Book and your word, even discipline in prayer itself, must all go for nothing, unless they make our daily life at work, on the streets of men, in the home, more like the life of Jesus in his love.

Save us from being religious in church, and at the same time cross, ill-tempered, moody, difficult to live with at home.

Save us from being meticulous in Bible study and in prayer, and at the same time slack, careless and inefficient at our work.

24

Save us from going through all the motions of religion on
Sunday, and at the same time being self-centred, bitter,
unforgiving, intolerant, proud, careless of the feelings
and the needs of others on Monday.

So cleanse and purify us that, not only our outward actions, but even the inmost thoughts of our hearts may be
pure. So remake us that we may not only not do any wrong
thing, but that we not even want to do it.
All this we ask through Jesus Christ our Lord. Amen.

The Circumcision is commemorated on 1st *January.*

25

The Epiphany, or the Manifestation of Christ to the Gentiles

O God, who by the leading of a star didst manifest thy only-begotten Son to the Gentiles: Mercifully grant, that we, which know thee now by faith, may after this life have the fruition of thy glorious Godhead; through Jesus Christ our Lord. Amen.

Epistle: Ephesians 3.1-12   *Gospel:* Matthew 2.1-12

O God, our Father, who in the ancient days led men from the ends of the earth to the manger-cradle of Jesus, your Son, our Lord, we know that you want all men to be saved. We know that Jesus said that, if he was lifted up from the earth, he would draw all men to him. Grant that the time may soon come when all men of every race and nation will know you and love you and serve you.

We thank you that we have been brought up in a land in which the Bible is open to us and in which the Church welcomes us, in which we possess liberty of conscience and freedom of speech and worship.

Help us always to remember those who do not possess the blessings which we enjoy:

Those who have never heard the name of Jesus;

Those who have had the glimpses of the light which all men have, but who have never seen him who is the true light of the world;

Those who live in lands where there is no freedom, and where they are persecuted for their faith.

Bless those who have gone out to take Christ to all such places.

> In their loneliness, cheer them;
> In their dangers, protect them;
> In their discouragements, give them unconquerable hope;
> And, if they have had to leave behind them wife and child and family in order to go out into the distant places, give them joy in your own presence and company.

Help us who remain at home to be ungrudging in giving and unwearied in service that those who have gone out may be supported in their God-given task of spreading your gospel among men.

So bring nearer the day when all men will know you and love you; when the knowledge of you will cover the earth as the waters cover the sea; when the kingdoms of the world will be your kingdom and the kingdom of your Christ.

This we ask through Jesus Christ our Lord. Amen.

The First Sunday after the Epiphany

O Lord, we beseech thee mercifully to receive the prayers of thy people which call upon thee; and grant that they may both perceive and know what things they ought to do, and also may have grace and power faithfully to fulfil the same; through Jesus Christ our Lord. Amen.

Epistle: Romans 12.1-5   *Gospel:* Luke 2.41-52

O God, our Father, give us wisdom to know what we ought to do.

Save us from
>   The cowardice which will not face the truth;
>   The laziness which will not learn the truth;
>   The prejudice which cannot see the truth;
>   The stubbornness which will not accept the truth;
>   The pride which will not seek the truth.

Save us from
>   The folly that is deaf to conscience;
>   The arrogance which will not accept advice;
>   The self-conceit which resents all rebuke;
>   The shut mind that bars the door to the entry of the Holy Spirit, who is the Spirit of truth.

O God, our Father, give us grace and power to do what we ought to do.

Save us from
>   The weakness of will which is too easily deflected from its goal;

28

The lack of resistance which too easily yields to temptation;

The procrastination which puts things off until it is too late to do them;

The want of perseverance which begins a task but cannot finish it.

Save us from

The love of ease which chooses the comfortable way;

The fear of men which cannot stand alone;

The faint heart which will not venture for your name.

So grant us wisdom clearly to know and power faithfully to fulfil your commands; through Jesus Christ our Lord. Amen.

The Second Sunday after the Epiphany

Almighty and everlasting God, who dost govern all things in heaven and earth: Mercifully hear the supplications of thy people, and grant us thy peace all the days of our life; through Jesus Christ our Lord. Amen.

Epistle: Romans 12.6-16   *Gospel:* John 2.1-11

Father of peace and God of love, grant us your peace.

Send your peace to the world.

Take from the world the threat of war, and bring in the time when the nations will live in friendship with each other, united as subjects of that Kingdom of which you are King, and as members of that Family of which you are Father. Give us strength and grace, faith and courage to build a world in which there are no national barriers, no political divisions, no iron curtains, no dividing walls, no colour bar, but in which men are one in Jesus Christ.

Send your peace to our country.

In politics help men to set the state above the party, and to set your will above all else.

In industry take away all suspicion and distrust. Put into men's minds the pride of craftsmanship and the desire to be workmen who have never any need to be ashamed of their work. Make employers to see their responsibilities to their employees, and make employees to see their duty to their employers, that all may work in brotherhood together for the common good.

Send peace within ourselves.

Help us to live in peace with our fellow men.

Rid us of the bitter and the unforgiving spirit. Control our temper and our tongue. Grant that we may nourish no grudge within our hearts and no memory of injury within our minds, and grant that brotherly love may banish hate.

Give us within our own hearts the peace that passes understanding.

Take from us the worries which distract us, and give us more trust.

Take from us the doubts which disturb us, and make us more sure of what we believe.

Take from us the wrong desires from which our temptations come, and make us more pure in heart.

Take from us the false ambitions which drive us, and make us more content to serve you where we are and as we are.

Take from us all estrangement from you and give us the peace of sins forgiven.

All this we ask through Jesus Christ our Lord. Amen.

Almighty and everlasting God, mercifully look upon our infirmities, and in all our dangers and necessities stretch forth thy right hand to help and defend us; through Jesus Christ our Lord. Amen.

Epistle: Romans 12.16-21   *Gospel:* Matthew 8.1-13

O God, our Father, we know so well the infirmity and the weakness of this human life.

> Strengthen the weakness of our faith, and give us trust for our trembling and hope for our fears.
> Strengthen the weakness of our wills, that we may ever be strong enough to choose the right and to resist the wrong.
> Strengthen the weakness of our decision, that we may no longer halt between two opinions.
> Strengthen the weakness of our loyalty, that we may never again be ashamed to show whose we are and whom we serve.
> Strengthen the weakness of our love, that we may come at last to love you as you have first loved us.

O God, our Father, we know so well the weakness of our bodies.

> Keep us in good health; but, if illness and pain come to us, give us patience and cheerful endurance and healing in the end. And, as the years take from us strength of body, give us peace of heart and serenity of mind.

O God, our Father, we know so well the weakness and the insecurity of our hold upon this life.

In life we are in the midst of death. Comfort us when dear and loved ones are taken from us, and at such a time give us the glorious and immortal hope of life eternal as well as the sad memories of mortal loss. And deliver us from the fear of death, so that we may look on death as the gateway to eternal life for ever with our Lord.

Grant us all through life your all-sufficient grace that your power may ever be made perfect in our weakness; through Jesus Christ our Lord. Amen.

The Fourth Sunday after the Epiphany

O God, who knowest us to be set in the midst of so many and great dangers, that by reason of the frailty of our nature we cannot always stand upright: Grant to us such strength and protection, as may support us in all dangers, and carry us through all temptations; through Jesus Christ our Lord. Amen.

Epistle: Romans 13.1-7   *Gospel:* Matthew 8.23-34

O God, our Father, help us to resist the temptations which continually attack us.

Help us to resist the temptations which come from within and from our own natures:

The temptation to laziness and to too much love of ease and comfort;

The temptation to pride and self-conceit and to think of ourselves more highly than we ought;

The temptation to put things off until it is too late ever to do them, and to refuse to face the unpleasant things, until it is too late to do anything about them:
Help us to resist these, O God.

The temptation to despair, and to lose heart and hope;

The temptation to lower our standards and to accept things as they are;

The temptation to be resignedly content with life as it is and ourselves as we are:
Help us to resist these, O God.

34

The temptation to let passion and desire have their
way;

The temptation to trade eternal happiness for the fleet-
ing thrill of some seductive moment;

The temptation to moodiness, to irritability, to bad
temper;

The temptation to criticism, to fault-finding, to thinking the worst of others:

Help us to resist these, O God.

Help us to resist the temptations which come to us from
outside.

Help us to say No to every voice which invites us to
leave your way.

Help us to resist every seduction which makes sin
more attractive.

Help us to walk through the world, and yet to keep
our garments unspotted from the world.

Help us to be wise enough never to play with fire; never to
flirt with temptation; never recklessly to put ourselves into
a situation in which it is easy to go wrong; never unthink-
ingly to develop habits which provide an opportunity for
sin.

Grant unto us that grace which will give us the strength and
the purity ever to overcome evil and to do the right; through
Jesus Christ our Lord. Amen.

The Fifth Sunday after the Epiphany

O Lord, we beseech thee to keep thy Church and household continually in thy true religion; that they who do lean only upon the hope of thy heavenly grace may evermore be defended by thy mighty power; through Jesus Christ our Lord. Amen.

Epistle: Colossians 3.12-17   *Gospel:* Matthew 13.24-30

O God, our Father, bless your Church,

> Give her such a passion for the souls of men, that she will never be content until all men shall know your love in Jesus Christ.
>
> Give her such a passion for social justice that she will ever be the conscience of the nation, and that she will engage upon a continuous crusade for everything that will benefit the bodies as well as the souls of men. Give her the conviction that each day is the Lord's Day, and so grant that she may be involved in every day's work and not only in one day's worship.
>
> Give her the adventurous spirit which refuses to be shackled to the past and which finds in tradition, not a deadweight, but an inspiration.
>
> Make her adventurous in thought that she may rethink and restate the eternal gospel in terms that men can understand.

Make her adventurous in action, so that she may not
  shrink from that which is new, and so that she may
  not rest content in a comfortable inertia.
Make her a fellowship in which all social and racial
  distinctions have ceased to exist.
Give her that true sympathy and tolerance which recognize that there are as many ways to the stars as there
  are men to climb them.
Give her at last that unity in which all barriers are
  broken down, in which all men can worship together
  again, and in which the body of Christ will be truly
  one.

Grant that the Church may be a place where boys and girls
find Jesus as their friend; where young men and maidens
glimpse the vision splendid; where those in the midtime find
a rod and a staff for the dust and the heat of the day; where
those far down the vale of years find light at eventide; where
the sorrowing find comfort and the weary rest; where the
doubting find certainty and the tempted strength; where the
lonely find fellowship and the sinner forgiveness for his sins.

Hear this our prayer, through Jesus Christ our Lord. Amen.

O God, whose blessed Son was manifested that he might destroy the works of the devil, and make us the sons of God, and heirs of eternal life: Grant us, we beseech thee, that, having this hope, we may purify ourselves, even as he is pure; that, when he shall appear again with power and great glory, we may be made like unto him in his eternal and glorious kingdom; where with thee, O Father, and thee, O Holy Ghost, he liveth and reigneth, ever one God, world without end. Amen.

Epistle: I John 3.1-8   *Gospel:* Matthew 24.23-31

O God, our Father, we thank you for Jesus Christ our Lord, and for the great hope that he has given to us.

 For the victory he has won;
  That he himself defeated the attacks of the Tempter,
   And that he can enable us also
   To overcome evil and to do the right;
 For the sonship that he has given to us;
  That he has brought us within your household and
   your family;
 For the life he has opened to us;
  That in this world
   He has given us life and life more abundant,
  That in the world to come
   He has promised us everlasting life:
     We thank you, O God.

Grant to us the purity which is his.

Grant that
He may reign within our hearts,
So that every evil emotion and desire
May be banished from them;
He may direct our minds,
So that all our thoughts may be right;
He may govern our actions,
So that we may do no wrong thing;
He may control our speech,
So that we may speak no word
Which is evil, false or impure.

So grant that, victorious with his victory, pure with his purity, and living with his life, we may not be ashamed at his appearing.

This we ask for your love's sake. Amen.

The Sunday called Septuagesima, or the Third Sunday before Lent

O Lord, we beseech thee favourably to hear the prayers of thy people; that we, who are justly punished for our offences, may be mercifully delivered by thy goodness, for the glory of thy Name; through Jesus Christ our Saviour, who liveth and reigneth with thee and the Holy Ghost, ever one God, world without end. Amen.

Epistle: I Corinthians 9.24-27   *Gospel:* Matthew 20.1-16

O God, you are the King and the Judge of all the earth. You are altogether good and altogether pure. We are stained with sin, lost in error, sunk in failure. If you were to give us what we deserve, we could expect nothing but condemnation, nothing but punishment, nothing but banishment for ever from your sight.

We have disobeyed your commandments,
    And have taken our own way;
The voice of conscience has spoken,
    And we have disregarded it;
We have seen the example of good and godly men,
    And we have not followed it;
We have received the advice and the counsel, the warning and the rebuke of those who are wise,
    And we have spurned them;
Experience has shown us the damage that self-will can do,
    And we have not learned from it;

We have wished to rule,
    And not to serve;
We have wished to avenge ourselves,
    And not to forgive;
We have wished to get,
    And not to give;
We have been silent,
    When we should have spoken;
We have rushed into speech,
    When we should have been silent;
We have been selfish and unkind in our homes;
    We have been slack and inefficient in our work;
We have been careless and irresponsible in our pleasure;
    We have been cold and neglectful in our devotion;
We have known what is right,
    And we have done what is wrong.

But we know that you are not only just and holy, but that you are also kind. Forgive us, not because of our merit, for we have none, but because of your love. Forgive us, not because of our goodness, for we have none, but because of your mercy. Take us just as we are, and forgive us for the past, and recreate us for the future. We only dare to ask this because of the love you have shown us in Jesus Christ our Saviour and our Blessed Lord.

Hear this our prayer for your love's sake. Amen.

The Sunday called Sexagesima, or the Second Sunday before Lent

O Lord God, who seest that we put not our trust in any thing that we do: Mercifully grant that by thy power we may be defended against all adversity; through Jesus Christ our Lord. Amen.

Epistle: II Corinthians 11.19-31   *Gospel:* Luke 8.4-15

O God, our Father, we know that by ourselves we can do nothing.

>If we try to face our work by ourselves,
>>we collapse beneath our burdens and our responsibilities. Our bodies become exhausted; our minds grow weary; our nerves are tensed beneath the strain.
>
>If we try to face our temptations by ourselves,
>>the fascination of the wrong things is too strong. Our resistance is defeated, and we do the things we know that we should never do, because we cannot help it.
>
>If we try to face our sorrows by ourselves,
>>there is nothing to heal the wound upon our hearts, nothing to dry the fountain of our tears, nothing to comfort the loneliness which is more than we can bear.
>
>If we try to face our problems by ourselves,
>>we cannot see the right way; and, even when we see it, we cannot take it; and, even when we take it, we cannot follow it to the end.

If we try to rid ourselves of faults by ourselves,
    we are for ever defeated; the same sins conquer
    us; and we are never any farther on.

We know our need. Life has taught us that we cannot walk
alone. So be with us to help, to guide, to comfort, to sustain,
that in all the changes and the chances of life, whatever
light may shine or shadow fall, we may meet life with steady
eyes, and walk in wisdom and in strength, in purity and in
joy in the way everlasting, until we reach our journey's end;
through Jesus Christ our Lord. Amen.

The Sunday called Quinquagesima, or the Next Sunday before Lent

O Lord, who hast taught us that all our doings without charity are nothing worth: Send thy Holy Ghost and pour into our hearts that most excellent gift of charity, the very bond of peace and of all virtues, without which whosoever liveth is counted dead before thee; Grant this for thine only Son Jesus Christ's sake. Amen.

Epistle: I Corinthians 13   *Gospel:* Luke 18.31-43

Eternal and ever blessed God, whose name is love, put your own love into our hearts; and help us to love you as you have first loved us.

> Help us to love you so much, that we may fear nothing except to grieve you and that we may desire nothing except to please you.
>
> Help us to love you so much, that we may obey you, not as a slave obeys his master, not even as a soldier obeys his commander, but as a loved one obeys his lover.
>
> Help us to love you so much, that the worship of your house may be to us neither a burden or a duty, but a joy and a delight.
>
> Help us to love you so much in answer to your love for us, that we too may say:
>> Were the whole realm of nature mine,
>>> That were an offering far too small;
>> Love so amazing, so divine,
>>> Demands my life, my soul, my all.

Help us, O Lover of the souls of men, to love our fellow men as you love them.

Help us to love them so much, that we shall always be ready to help and always quick to forgive.

Help us to love them so much, that hatred and bitterness may no longer have any place within our hearts.

Help us to love them so much, that all men shall know that we are your disciples, because we have love one for another.

All this we ask for your love's sake. Amen.

The First Day of Lent, commonly called Ash-Wednesday

Almighty and everlasting God, who hatest nothing that thou hast made, and dost forgive the sins of all them that are penitent: Create and make in us new and contrite hearts, that we worthily lamenting our sins, and acknowledging our wretchedness, may obtain of thee, the God of all mercy, perfect remission and forgiveness; through Jesus Christ our Lord. Amen.

Lesson: Joel 2.12-17   *Gospel:* Matthew 6.16-21

O God, Creator and Father of all, we know that your love is over every creature whom your hands have made. We know that your only wish is not to destroy but to save, not to condemn but to forgive. And we know that, if we would receive your forgiveness, the only thing that we can bring, and the only thing that we need to bring, to you is the penitent and the contrite heart. Save us from everything which would hinder us from having a godly sorrow for our sins.

> Save us, O God,
> > From the blindness,
> > > which is not even aware that it is sinning;
> > From the pride,
> > > which cannot admit that it is wrong;
> > From the self-will,
> > > which can see nothing but its own way;
> > From the self-righteousness,
> > > which can see no flaw within itself;

46

From the callousness,
> which has sinned so often that it has ceased to
> care;

From the defiance,
> which is not even sorry for its sins;

From the evasion,
> which always puts the blame on some one or on
> some thing else;

From the heart so hardened,
> that it cannot repent.

Give us at all times
> Eyes which are open to our own faults;
> A conscience which is sensitive and quick to warn;
> A heart which cannot sin in peace,
>> but which is moved to regret and to remorse.

So grant that being truly penitent we may be truly forgiven, so that we may find that your love is great enough to cover all our sin; through Jesus Christ our Lord. Amen.

The Ash-Wednesday Collect is used throughout Lent.

The First Sunday in Lent

O Lord, who for our sake didst fast forty days and forty nights: Give us grace to use such abstinence, that, our flesh being subdued to the Spirit, we may ever obey thy godly motions in righteousness, and true holiness, to thy honour and glory, who livest and reignest with the Father and the Holy Ghost, one God, world without end. Amen.

Epistle: II Corinthians 6.1-10   *Gospel:* Matthew 4.1-11

O Lord Jesus Christ, give us in all our life the discipline which will enable us to walk in your footsteps, and which all your true followers should show.

> Help us to discipline our passions and desires, that we may never in an unguarded moment do that which we would afterwards regret.
>
> Help us to discipline our appetites, that greed and gluttony and self-indulgence may have no part in our lives.
>
> Help us to discipline our speech, that no false or untrue word, no soiled or impure word, no bitter or angry word may ever pass our lips.
>
> Help us to discipline ourselves in our work, that slackness, idleness, laziness and carelessness may find no place in our lives, that we may not try to find how quickly we can do a thing but how well we can do it, that we may be more concerned with how much we can put into a task than with how much we can get out of it.

Help us to discipline ourselves in our pleasure, that no pleasure may ever so master us that it takes away the will-power to resist it.

Help us to discipline ourselves in our devotion, that we may faithfully share in the public worship of your people, and that no day may ever pass when in the silence we do not speak and listen to you.

Help us to discipline even our thoughts, that they may never move in any forbidden pathways or linger on any forbidden thing, so that we too may be pure in heart and so see you.

This we ask for your love's sake. Amen.

The Second Sunday in Lent

Almighty God, who seest that we have no power of our-selves to help ourselves: Keep us both outwardly in our bodies, and inwardly in our souls; that we may be defended from all adversities which may happen to the body, and from all evil thoughts which may assault and hurt the soul; through Jesus Christ our Lord. Amen.

Epistle: I Thessalonians 4.1-8   *Gospel:* Matthew 15.21-28

O God, our Father, you have shown us in the works and words of Jesus, your Son, that you care both for our bodies and our souls. Protect us alike in body and in soul.

We pray for your blessing on our bodies.
>Health for our day's work;
>Wisdom to seek the doctor's skill, if we know, or even suspect, that anything is wrong;
>Wisdom neither to overdrive our bodies until we ex-haust them, nor to allow them to grow weak and flabby through too much ease;
>Wise discipline in our habits, that we may allow ourselves no indulgences nor become the victim of any habits which would injure our health:
>>Grant this, O God.

And since we know that mind and body are linked in-separably together, grant us a sound mind:
>A mind at rest and at peace;
>A mind undistressed by worry, and free from anxiety;

A mind cleansed and purified from every evil, every
bitter and every resentful thought;
A mind determined to do all it can, and then content
to leave the rest to you:
Grant this, O God.

We pray for your blessing on our souls.
From being so immersed in the world that we forget
that we have a soul;
From being so busy with the things which are seen
and temporal that we entirely forget the things
which are unseen and eternal;
From forgetting that it does not profit us if we gain
the whole world if in so doing we lose our soul:
Save us, O God.

From the temptations which attack our soul from inside and from outside;
From all habits and practices and ways of life which
make our soul less sensitive to you;
From all that makes our soul less fit to enter your
presence when this life ends:
Defend us, O God.

Bless us in body, soul and spirit that we may live this life
well, and at the end of it enter into life eternal; through
Jesus Christ our Lord. Amen.

The Third Sunday in Lent

We beseech thee, Almighty God, look upon the hearty desires of thy humble servants, and stretch forth the right hand of thy Majesty, to be our defence against all our enemies; through Jesus Christ our Lord. Amen.

Epistle: Ephesians 5.1-14   *Gospel:* Luke 11.14-28

O God, you are the help of the helpless. You can cover our defenceless head with the shadow of your wing. It is for your defence and protection that we ask today

Defend us from our temptations,
>That in your power,
>>We may ever accept the right and refuse the wrong,
>>We may ever overcome all evil and do the right.

Defend us from ourselves
>That in your power,
>>Our weaknesses may not bring us to shame,
>>Our lower nature may never seize the upper hand.

Defend us from all that would seduce us into sin,
>That in your power,
>>No tempting voice may make us listen,
>>No tempting sight may fascinate our eyes.

Defend us against the changes and the chances of this life,
>Not that we may escape them,
>>But that we may meet them with head erect and with steady eyes;

Not that we may be saved from then,
>   But that we may come triumphantly through
>   them.

Defend us alike
>   From discouragement in difficulty, and from despair
>   in failure;
>   From pride in success and from forgetting you in the
>   day of prosperity.

Help us to remember that
>   There is no time,
>   >   When you will fail us,
>   And no moment,
>   >   When we do not need you.

So grant that guided by your light and defended by your grace we may come in safety and in honour to our journey's end; through Jesus Christ our Lord. Amen.

The Fourth Sunday in Lent

Grant, we beseech thee, Almighty God, that we, who for our evil deeds do worthily deserve to be punished, by the comfort of thy grace may mercifully be relieved; through our Lord and Saviour Jesus Christ. Amen.

Epistle: Galatians 4.21-31   *Gospel:* John 6.1-14

O God, we thank you that you have not treated us as we deserve.

We thank you that, though you are Creator, Judge and King, you are also Father, so that, though we are wandering children, there is always a road back to our Father's house.

You have spoken to us,
  In the voice of conscience,
  In the words of your Book,
  In the promptings of your Holy Spirit,
    And yet we have not obeyed your voice.

You have shown us the best,
  In the ideals which still haunt us,
  In the life and example of godly men,
  In the pattern of Jesus,
    And yet we have not followed it.

You have tried to teach us,
  In the events of history,
  In the experiences of life,

In the wisdom of the sages, the prophets and the saints,
>And yet we have not learned your lesson.

You have called us to the life of love,
>To the forgiving of each other,
>To the helping of those in need,
>To the caring which is like your care,
>>And yet we have lived in bitterness, in selfishness and in heedlessness of the appeal of need.

We have nothing in our hands to bring. We have no merits of our own. There is no plea of self-defence that we can offer. So above all else we thank you for Jesus Christ our Saviour, who died that we might be forgiven. So for his sake hear us as we say: God be merciful to me a sinner.

>And when you hear,
>Forgive and save.

This we ask for your love's sake. Amen.

The Fifth Sunday in Lent

We beseech thee, Almighty God, mercifully to look upon thy people; that by thy great goodness they may be governed and preserved evermore, both in body and soul; through Jesus Christ our Lord. Amen.

Epistle: Hebrews 9.11-15   *Gospel:* John 8.46-59

O God, our Father, direct and control us in every part of our life.

> Control our tongues,
>> that we may speak no false, no angry, no impure word.

> Control our actions,
>> that we may do nothing to shame ourselves or to injure anyone else.

> Control our minds,
>> that we may think no evil, no bitter, no irreverent thought.

> Control our hearts,
>> that they may never be set on any wrong thing, and that they may ever love only the highest and the best.

O God, our Father, to whom the issues of life and death belong, preserve us from all ills.

> Preserve us in health of body,
>> that we may be able to earn a living for ourselves and for those whom we love.

56

Preserve us in soundness of mind,
> that all our judgments and decisions may be sane and wise.

Preserve us in purity of life,
> that we may conquer all temptation and ever do the right,
>
> that we may walk through the world and yet keep our garments unspotted from the world.

And if illness, misfortune, sorrow come to us, preserve us in courage, in endurance, and in serenity of faith, that, in all the changes and the chances of life, we may still face life with steady eyes, because we face life with you.

This we ask for your love's sake. Amen.

The Sunday, Monday, Tuesday, Wednesday and Thursday before Easter

Almighty and everlasting God, who, of thy tender love towards mankind, hast sent thy Son, our Saviour, Jesus Christ, to take upon him our flesh, and to suffer death upon the cross, that all mankind should follow the example of his great humility: Mercifully grant, that we may follow the example of his patience and also be made partakers of his resurrection; through the same Jesus Christ our Lord. Amen.

Sunday

Epistle: Philippians 2.5-11   *Gospel:* Matthew 27.1-54

Monday

Lesson: Isaiah 63   *Gospel:* Mark 14

Tuesday

Lesson: Isaiah 50.5-11   *Gospel:* Mark 15.1-39

Wednesday

Epistle: Hebrews 9.16-28   *Gospel:* Luke 22

Thursday

Epistle: I Corinthians 11.17-34   *Gospel:* Luke 23.1-49

Eternal and everblessed God, you sent your Son Jesus into the world to be an example to us. Help us ever to walk in his steps.

Help us to walk
  In his humility,
    So that we too may be among our fellow men as those who serve;

  In his forgiveness,
    So that we too may forgive, as we hope to be forgiven;

Help us to walk
  In his courage,
    So that nothing may ever deflect us from the way we ought to take;

  In his endurance,
    So that nothing may daunt or discourage us, until we reach our goal;

  In his loyalty,
    So that nothing may ever seduce our hearts from our devotion to him.

Help us to share the life that our Lord once lived on earth that we may also share the life he lives in his risen power.

  Grant that it may be our meat and drink to do the will of our Father who is in heaven.

  Grant unto us to take up whatever cross is laid upon us and gallantly and gladly to carry it.

  Grant that
    As we may share his cross,
    So we may share his crown;
    As we share his death,
    So we may also share his life.

And so grant that having suffered with him we may also reign with him.

This we ask for your love's sake. Amen.

Good Friday

1

Almighty God, we beseech thee graciously to behold this thy family, for which our Lord Jesus Christ was contented to be betrayed, and given up into the hands of wicked men, and to suffer death upon the cross, who now liveth and reigneth with thee and the Holy Ghost, ever one God, world without end. Amen.

O God of love, we remember today all that our blessed Lord endured for us.

> Let us remember how Jesus was betrayed, and given up into the hands of wicked men.

Lord Jesus, we remember today that it was one of your own familiar friends who betrayed you, and we know that there is nothing which so breaks the heart as the disloyalty of one whom we called friend. Grant that we may not betray you. Save us,

> From the cowardice,
>> which would disown you when it is hard to be true to you;
>
> From the disloyalty,
>> which betrays you in the hour when you need some one to stand by you;
>
> From the fickleness,
>> which blows hot and cold in its devotion;
>
> From the fair-weather friendship,
>> which, when things are difficult or dangerous,
>>> makes us ashamed to show whose we are and whom we serve.

Let us remember how Jesus suffered death upon the Cross.

Lord Jesus, help us to remember

    The lengths to which your love was ready to go;

    That having loved your own you loved them to the very end;

    The love than which none can be greater, the love which lays down its life for its friends;

    That it was while men were yet enemies that you died for them.

Let us remember how Jesus now lives and reigns.

Help us to remember

    That the Crucified Lord is the Risen Lord;

    That the Cross has become the Crown.

So grant unto us,

    To trust in his love;

    To live in his presence;

    That we may share in his glory.

This we ask for your love's sake. Amen

2

Almighty and everlasting God, by whose Spirit the whole body of the Church is governed and sanctified: Receive our supplications and prayers, which we offer before thee for all estates of men in thy holy Church, that every member of the same, in his vocation and ministry, may truly and godly serve thee; through our Lord and Saviour Jesus Christ. Amen.

Lord Jesus, King and Head of the Church, today we ask you to bless all those who do any work within your Church.

> Those who preach,
> > that they may have,
> > > your truth in their minds;
> > > your love in their hearts;
> > > your eloquence on their lips.

> Those who teach,
> > that they themselves may know as Saviour and Lord that Jesus whom they seek to introduce to others.

> Those who are leaders of the youth organizations,
> > that they may attract others to you
> > > by the strength and beauty of their own lives.

> Those who serve on the Church's committees and lead in the Church's organizations, societies and activities,
> > that they may hold back none of their talents,
> > > and that they may allow nothing to disturb their fellowship.

Those who sing and those who make music,
>   that their praise may come from hearts that love you,
>   so that their work may not be a performance but
>   an act of worship.

Those whose duty it is to administer the affairs of the Church,
>   that they may faithfully, wisely and lovingly
>   care for the things of your house and your household.

Those whose task it is to keep clean and fresh and tidy the church and its premises,
>   that they may find joy even in these common tasks;
>   and make others thoughtful enough not to make the work of all such harder than it need be.

All who come to worship and to learn each Sunday,
and to be happy in fellowship in the days of the week;
and grant that every congregation of Christian people may be a place where people find each other and find you.

All this we ask for your love's sake. Amen.

Good Friday

O merciful God, who hast made all men, and who hatest nothing that thou hast made, nor wouldest the death of a sinner, but rather that he should be converted and live: Have mercy upon all Jews, Turks, Infidels, and Hereticks, and take from them all ignorance, hardness of heart, and contempt of thy Word; and so fetch them home, blessed Lord, to thy flock, that they may be saved among the remnant of the true Israelites, and be made one fold under one shepherd, Jesus Christ our Lord, who liveth and reigneth with thee and the Holy Spirit, one God, world without end. Amen.

Epistle: Hebrews 10.1-25   *Gospel:* John 19.1-37

O God, you are the Father of all men, and you can never be content until all your children come home to you, and until your family is complete. We ask you to put into our hearts your own concern for those who still do not know you and love you.

Give us patience and skill,
>to appeal to those whose hearts are hard, and whose minds are shut.

Give us wisdom and understanding,
>to enlighten those who do not know the truth.

Help us to prove
>the worth, the value, the power of your word to those who despise it, not only by the arguments of our

words but by the quality of our life. Help us so to live that they will be compelled to see that we have a secret they do not possess.

Fill us with missionary desire to win those who have never heard the message of the Christian faith, and give us such a grasp of the truth, and such a skill to commend it and defend it, that we may be able to counsel, convince and persuade those who have refused it or misunderstood it or perverted it.

So grant that the day may quickly come when all men will be united in the one family of which you are the Head and in the one flock of which Jesus Christ is the Chief Shepherd, the day when the knowledge of you shall cover the earth as the waters cover the sea, the day when all men shall know you and love you from the least to the greatest, the day when the kingdoms of the world will be the Kingdom of the Lord; through Jesus Christ our Lord. Amen.

Easter Even

Grant, O Lord, that as we are baptized into the death of thy blessed Son our Saviour Jesus Christ, so by continual mortifying our corrupt affections we may be buried with him; and that through the grave, and gate of death, we may pass to our joyful resurrection; for his merits, who died, and was buried, and rose again for us, thy Son Jesus Christ our Lord. Amen.

Epistle: I Peter 3.17-22   *Gospel:* Matthew 27.57-66

O God, grant to us to share in the life and the death and the resurrection of our Lord Jesus Christ.

> Grant that through him and with him we may die to sin and live to righteousness.

> Grant that through him and with him our old self may die, and a new self, victorious over sin and lovely with goodness, may be created.

> Grant that through him and with him we may become a new creation in which the old things have passed away, and in which everything has become new.

So grant that even here and now we may die to sin and be reborn to goodness.

And grant that we may be so one with our risen Lord that, when life ends for us in this world, we may know that death is the gateway to eternal life.

> Make us quite certain that, if a man dies, he will live again.

Deliver us from the fear of death; and make us to know that death is not the end but the beginning of life, not the twilight but the dawn, not the midnight but the breaking day.

So grant us the certainty that beyond death there is a life,

Where the broken things are mended,
And the lost things found;
Where there is rest for the weary,
And joy for the sad;
Where all we have hoped and willed of good
Shall exist;
Where the dream will come true,
And the ideal will be realized;
Where we shall be for ever with our Lord.

So grant us the Easter certainty that life is stronger than death; through Jesus Christ our Lord. Amen.

Easter-Day

Almighty God, who through thine only-begotten Son Jesus Christ hast overcome death, and opened unto us the gate of everlasting life: we humbly beseech thee, that, as by thy special grace preventing us thou dost put into our minds good desires, so by thy continual help we may bring the same to good effect; through Jesus Christ our Lord, who liveth and reigneth with thee and the Holy Ghost, ever one God, world without end. Amen.

Epistle: Colossians 3.1-7   *Gospel:* John 20.1-10

O God, our Father, you have put immortal longings into the hearts of men, and we thank you for them.

> For the ideals which haunt us;
> For the noble desires which move us to long for good-
> ness;
> For the high ambitions to make life a shining thing:
> > We thank you, O God.

Forgive us, O God, for everything that keeps us from making the ideal into the real.

> For the laziness that will not make an effort;
> For the idleness which loves to do nothing;
> For the procrastination which puts things off until it is
> too late ever to do them;
> For the lack of perseverance which gives up too easily
> and too soon:
> > Forgive us, O God.

Grant unto us, God, all that we need to make the dream come true.

> Strength of will;
> Steadiness of purpose;
> Ability to do;
> Willingness to bear:
> > Grant us this, O God.

> Wisdom to see what we ought to do;
> Courage to begin it;
> Fidelity to continue it;
> Strength and skill to complete it:
> > Grant us this, O God.

And even if we begin and fail, help us to know that it is better to attempt and to fail in some great thing rather than not to try at all.

So grant unto us the vision, and the power to make the vision into a deed; through Jesus Christ our Lord. Amen.

Almighty God, who through thy only-begotten Son Jesus Christ hast overcome death, and opened unto us the gate of everlasting life: We humbly beseech thee, that, as by thy special grace preventing us thou dost put into our minds good desires, so by thy continual help we may bring the same to good effect; through Jesus Christ our Lord, who liveth and reigneth with thee and the Holy Ghost, ever one God, world without end. Amen.

Monday

Lesson: Acts 10.34-43   *Gospel:* Luke 24.13-35

Tuesday

Lesson: Acts 13.26-41   *Gospel:* Luke 24.36-48

O God, our Father, at Easter time we remember the great hope of eternal life which you have set before us, and we feel within our hearts the longings for goodness and for you. Grant that nothing may hinder the hope of eternal life from coming true, and the desire for goodness and for you from being realized.

Grant, O God,
    That we may never lose the way through our self-will,
        and so end up in the far countries of the soul;
    That we may never abandon the struggle,
        but that we may endure to the end,
        and so be saved;

That we may never drop out of the race,
  but that we may ever press forward
  to the goal of our high calling;
That we may never choose the cheap and passing
things,
  and let go the precious things that last for ever;
That we may never take the easy way,
  and so leave the right way;
That we may never forget
  that sweat is the price of all things,
  and that without the cross, there cannot be the
  crown.

So keep us and strengthen us by your grace that no disobedience and no weakness and no failure may stop us from entering into the blessedness which awaits those who are faithful in all the changes and the chances of life down even to the gates of death; through Jesus Christ our Lord. Amen.

The First Sunday after Easter

Almighty Father, who hast given thine only Son to die for our sins, and to rise again for our justification: Grant us so to put away the leaven of malice and wickedness, that we may alway serve thee in pureness of living and truth; through the merits of the same thy Son Jesus Christ our Lord. Amen.

Epistle: I John 5.4-12   *Gospel:* John 20.19-23

O God, our Father, in the life and death and resurrection of Jesus you have given us the remedy for sin. In him you have opened to us the way to forgiveness for all our past sins, and you have given us the strength and the power to live in purity and in truth.

Help us to put away all evil things.
   Silence the evil word;
   Forbid the evil deed;
   Break the evil habit;
   Banish the evil thought;
   Take away the evil desire and the evil ambition;
      and make our lives to shine like lights
      in this dark world.

Help us to live in purity.
   Make all our words so pure
      that you may hear them;
   Make all our deeds so pure
      that you may see them;

Make all our thoughts and desires so pure
   that they may bear your scrutiny.
And so grant that we being pure in heart
   may see you.

Help us to live in truth.
   Grant
      That we may never speak or act a lie;
      That we may never be misled by false or mistaken
      beliefs;
      That we may never evade the truth,
         even when we do not want to see it.

Grant to us at all times
   To seek and to find;
   To know and to love;
   To obey and to live
      the truth.

This we ask for the sake of him who is the Way, the Truth
and the Life, even for the sake of Jesus Christ our Lord.
Amen.

The Second Sunday after Easter

Almighty God, who hast given thine only Son, to be unto us both a sacrifice for sin, and also an ensample of godly life: Give us grace that we may always most thankfully receive that his inestimable benefit, and also daily endeavour ourselves to follow the blessed steps of his most holy life; through the same Jesus Christ our Lord. Amen.

Epistle: I Peter 2.19-25   *Gospel:* John 10.11-16

O God, our Father, we thank you for Jesus Christ, your Son, our Lord.

We thank you for his sacrifice for us.
That he gave his life a ransom for many;
That he was obedient unto death, even the death of the Cross;
We thank you, O God.

We thank you for his example to us.
That he left us an example that we should follow in his steps;
That he is to us the Way, the Truth and the Life;
That in him you have shown us what is good:
We thank you, O God.

Help us to follow the example he has given us.

Help us to follow the example,
Of his courage,
that nothing may deflect us from the way we ought to take;

Of his humility,
   that in us too self may die;
Of his obedience,
   that for us too to do your will may be life itself;
Of his kindness,
   that we too may go about doing good;
Of his forgiveness,
      that we too may be tender-hearted, forgiving one
      another, even as you for his sake have forgiven
      us;
Of his love,
      that the last particle of hatred may be banished
      from our hearts and from our lives.

So grant that we may show that we are redeemed, so that
others may believe in our redeemer; through Jesus Christ
our Lord. Amen.

Almighty God, who showest to them that be in error the light of thy truth, to the intent that they may return into the way of righteousness: Grant unto all them that are admitted into the fellowship of Christ's Religion, that they may eschew those things which are contrary to their profession, and follow all such things as are agreeable to the same; through our Lord Jesus Christ. Amen.

Epistle: I Peter 2.11-17   *The Gospel:* John 16.16-22

O God, help us at all times to make our deeds fit our words, and to make our conduct match our profession; and grant that we may never say one thing with our lips and another with our lives.

Grant that we may not praise service and practise selfishness.

Grant that for us sympathy may never only be a thing of the emotions, but that it may always issue in action to help. Grant that, when we feel sorry for some one, we may not be satisfied until we have done something to help.

Grant that we may not praise love and practise bitterness.

Grant that we may not sing of the beauty of loving one another, and yet refuse to forgive one another. Grant that we may not dream of a time of brotherly love, and yet be unable to live at peace with our neighbour.

Grant that we may not praise honesty and practise falsehood.

Grant that we may not be guilty of the hypocrisy which says one thing with its lips and means another in its heart, and which is one thing to a person's face and another behind his back. Grant that we may not pay lip service to the truth, and yet be willing to evade, suppress, or twist the truth, when we think that it suits us to do so.

Grant that we may not praise generosity and practise meanness.

Keep us from the hypocrisy of singing hymns about giving everything to you, and then grudging every penny we give and every hour we devote to the service of your people and your Church.

Keep us, O God, from bringing discredit by our life and our actions, our words and our behaviour on the faith which we profess, the Church to which we belong, and the Master whom we ought to serve; through Jesus Christ our Lord. Amen.

The Fourth Sunday after Easter

*O Almighty God, who alone canst order the unruly wills
and affections of sinful men: Grant unto thy people, that
they may love the things which thou commandest, and
desire that which thou dost promise; that so, among the
sundry and manifold changes of the world, our hearts may
surely there be fixed, where true joys are to be found;
through Jesus Christ our Lord.* Amen.

Epistle: James 1.17-21   *Gospel:* John 16.5-15

O God, our Father, you gave us wills of our own that we
should make them yours. And yet there is in us a pride, a
self-will, a stubbornness, which make us impatient of all
control and determined on our own way.

Help us, O God, to remember what you are.

  Help us to remember
    Your wisdom,
      that we may never doubt,
        that you know best.

  Help us to remember
    Your love,
      that we may never doubt
        that you will seek only our good.

  Help us to remember
    Your power,
      that we may never doubt,
        that you can do all that you promise.

78

Grant that we may willingly and gladly obey you.
> Grant that we may seek,
>> Only to do your will;
>> Only to gladden your love;
>> Only to seek the rewards which you alone can give.

To that end take from us,
> The pride,
>> which will not surrender its will to you;
> The blindness,
>> which does not see the wonder of your love;
> The short sight,
>> which seizes the pleasure of a moment,
>>> and forfeits the eternal joy.

So grant that in your service we may find our perfect freedom, and in doing your will our peace; through Jesus Christ our Lord. Amen.

The Fifth Sunday after Easter

O Lord, from whom all good things do come: Grant to us thy humble servants, that by thy holy inspiration we may think those things that be good, and by thy merciful guiding may perform the same; through Jesus Christ our Lord. Amen.

Epistle: James 1.22-27   *Gospel:* John 16.23-33

O God, without you we can neither think nor act aright.

Help us to banish from our minds,
    All bitter thoughts,
      which would divide us from our fellow men;
    All proud thoughts,
      which would make us conceited and contemptuous of others,
        and which would make us think of our own place and prestige;
    All selfish thoughts,
      which would make us regardless of the needs and of the feelings of others;
    All impure thoughts,
      which would give temptation its chance,
        and which would leave a stain upon our minds.

Help us to banish from our lives,
    All careless work,
      which is not good enough to show to you;
    All cowardly action,
      which is afraid to show what it believes;

All thoughtless action,
>   which forgets to look at the consequences of what it does;

All rash action,
>   which is at the mercy of the impulse or the passion of the moment.

Help us to think
>   In purity and in love;

Help us to act
>   In honesty and honour.

Hear this our prayer; through Jesus Christ our Lord. Amen.

The Ascension Day

Grant, we beseech thee, Almighty God, that like as we do believe thy only-begotten Son our Lord Jesus Christ to have ascended into the heavens; so we may also in heart and mind thither ascend, and with him continually dwell, who liveth and reigneth with thee and the Holy Ghost, one God, world without end. Amen.

Lesson: Acts 1.1-11   *Gospel:* Mark 16.14-20

Eternal God, as today we remember that our Blessed Lord ascended up into heaven, help us to set our affections on the things that are above.

> Grant that your voice may speak to us
>> more compellingly than any earthly voice;
>
> Grant that your will may be dearer to us
>> than any earthly desires;
>
> Grant that your purpose may mean more to us
>> than any earthly ambition.
>
> Help us to judge things,
>> not in the light of time,
>> but in the light of eternity.
>
> Help us to value things,
>> not as men value them,
>> but as you value them;
>> and so to see that it will profit us nothing
>> to gain the whole world,
>> if in so doing we lose our soul.

Help us to see things,
  not as men see them,
  but as you see them;
  so that we may see
  what things are important,
  and what things do not matter,
  even if the world holds them dear.

Help us to act,
  not to please men,
  but to please you.

Help us to walk,
  not looking for the favour of men,
  but with our eyes steadfastly fixed on Jesus.

So grant that in the here and now we may always be conscious of the there and then, and that here in the present we may ever remember the things which are beyond; through Jesus Christ our Lord. Amen.

Sunday after Ascension-Day

O God, the King of glory, who hast exalted thine only Son Jesus Christ with great triumph unto thy kingdom in heaven: We beseech thee, leave us not comfortless; but send to us thine Holy Ghost to comfort us, and exalt us unto the same place whither our Saviour Christ is gone before, who liveth and reigneth with thee and the Holy Ghost, one God, world without end. Amen.

Epistle: I Peter 4.7-11   *Gospel:* John 15.26-16.4

O God, our Father, we remember that Jesus promised that he would send to us the Holy Spirit from you. Keep that promise to us today.

He called his Spirit the Spirit of truth.

Open our eyes that we may see the truth;

Strengthen our hearts that we may face the truth;

Enlighten our minds that we may understand the truth;

Make our memories retentive that we may remember the truth;

Make resolute our wills that we may obey the truth, through the Spirit which he has promised to us.

He said that the Spirit would bring to our remembrance all that he had said to men.

O God, when we are in danger of forgetting the things which we should always remember, grant that your Spirit may bring again to our memory the promises, the commands and the presence of our risen and blessed Lord.

He said that the Spirit would take what is his and declare it to us.

O God, when we do not know what to do, when we find the teachings of our Lord either difficult to understand or to apply, grant that your Spirit may show us what to believe and what to do.

He said that the Spirit would tell us things which in the days of his flesh he could not say to his disciples, because they were not ready to receive them.

O God, keep us from ever thinking of our Christian faith and belief as something static. Help us to remember that there are ever new depths of truth, new vistas of beauty, new glories of experience, new gifts of power into which the Spirit can lead us.

He said that the Spirit would lead us into all truth.

Help us to remember that all truth belongs to you—
The skill of the scientist and the thought of the philosopher;
The inspiration of the poet, the vision of the artist, the melody of the musician;
The craft of the craftsman and the strength of body and of mind by which we make a living.

And since everything comes from you, help us to use everything for you and for our fellow men; through Jesus Christ our Lord. Amen.

Whit-Sunday and Monday and Tuesday in Whitsun-Week

God, who as at this time didst teach the hearts of thy faithful people, by the sending to them the light of thy Holy Spirit: Grant us by the same Spirit to have a right judgement in all things, and evermore to rejoice in his holy comfort; through the merits of Jesus Christ our Saviour, who liveth and reigneth with thee, in the unity of the same Spirit, one God, world without end. Amen.

Whit-Sunday

Lesson: Acts 2.1-11   *Gospel:* John 14.15-31

Monday in Whitsun-Week

Lesson: Acts 10.34-48   *Gospel:* John 3.16-21

Tuesday in Whitsun-Week

Lesson: Acts 8.14-17   *Gospel:* John 10. 1-10

O God, our Father, give us your Holy Spirit in our hearts and in our minds that we may ever choose aright.

Give us your Holy Spirit that we may know,
    which way to choose, and which way to refuse;
    which choice to make, and which choice to reject;
    which course of action to take, and which course of action to avoid.

Give us your Holy Spirit,
    to enlighten our minds,
        to see what we ought to do;

    to strengthen our wills,
       to choose the right course of action,
         and to abide by it;
    to empower our lives,
       to follow the right way to the end.

Give us your Holy Spirit,
    to cleanse our minds of all evil and impure thoughts;
    to fill our hearts with all lovely and noble desires;
    to make our lives
       wise with knowledge,
       beautiful with love,
       useful with service.

Give us your Holy Spirit,
    to light up the pages of your Book for us;
    to teach us for what we ought to pray;
    to enrich our lives with the fruit which only he can give.

Grant us all this for your love's sake. Amen.

Trinity-Sunday

Almighty and everlasting God, who hast given unto us thy servants grace by the confession of a true faith to acknowledge the glory of the eternal Trinity, and in the power of the Divine Majesty to worship the Unity: We beseech thee, that thou wouldest keep us stedfast in this faith, and evermore defend us from all adversities, who livest and reignest, one God, world without end. Amen.

Lesson: Revelation 4.1-11   *Gospel:* John 3.1-14

Let us remember God in Creation

O God, the Father, we thank you for your creating power.

> That you have made all things and made them well;
> That you have given us all things richly to enjoy;
> For the beauty and the bounty of this fair earth;
> And for the creating power which can make all things new:
>> We thank you, O Father.

> Forgive us if in pride and selfishness and in anger we have misused your gifts, and have used for death that which was meant for life.

Let us remember God in Redemption

O Lord Jesus Christ the Son, we thank you for your redeeming power.

> That you loved us and gave yourself for us;
> That you gave your life a ransom for many, a ransom for us;

That you were obedient unto death, even the death of
the Cross:
> We thank you, O Christ.

Forgive us if we have treated your love lightly as a
little thing, and if we have never even begun to love
you as you have first loved us.

Let us remember God in Providence

O Holy Spirit of God, we thank you for your keeping power.

For the guidance you have given us;

For the knowledge you have brought us;

For your continual upholding, strengthening, protect-
ing power:
> We thank you, O Spirit of God.

Forgive us if we have tried to live life alone, and have
despoiled ourselves of the divine help we might have
had from you.

And may the blessing of God, the Father, the Son, and the
Holy Spirit, the Three in One, and the One in Three, be on
us now and stay with each one of us always. Amen.

The First Sunday after Trinity

O God, the strength of all them that put their trust in thee: Mercifully accept our prayers; and because through the weakness of our mortal nature we can do no good thing without thee, grant us the help of thy grace, that in keeping of thy commandments we may please thee, both in will and deed; through Jesus Christ our Lord. Amen.

Epistle: I John 4.7-21   *Gospel:* Luke 16.19-31

O God, our Father, we know our own weakness.

Our wills are weak.
    We know the right, and cannot do it.
    We make our resolutions, and cannot keep them.
    We see the ideal,
        but the byways are so fascinating,
        the uphill road is so difficult,
            that we lose the way.

Our passions are so strong.
    Our emotions are stronger than our wills.
    We are swept away by the passion of the moment.
    The sudden impulse will brook no denial.
        And we do,
            what we never meant to do,
            and what we regret doing.

We need your grace,
    Grace to overcome evil and to do the right,
    Grace to rid of ourselves of old faults, and to gain
        new virtues,

Grace,
To turn the vision into the deed,
To turn the ideal into the real,
To turn the dream into the action,
To do that which we already know we ought to do.

So grant that your grace may make our weakness strong,
So that we may overcome all evil,
So that without stumbling and without straying
we may walk stedfastly in the way everlasting,
So that we may obey your commandments,
So that we may at the last reach our journey's end in
honour and hear you say: Well done!

Hear this our prayer; through Jesus Christ our Lord. Amen.

O Lord, who never failest to help and govern them whom thou dost bring up in thy stedfast fear and love: Keep us, we beseech thee, under the protection of thy good providence, and make us to have a perpetual fear and love of thy holy Name; through Jesus Christ our Lord. Amen.

Epistle: I John 3.13-24   *Gospel:* Luke 14.16-24

Keep us, O God, for ever in your fear and in your love.

Grant us that godly fear,
    which will keep us from breaking your commandments;
    which will keep us from disobeying your law;
    which will keep us from refusing your guidance.
Grant us that godly fear,
    which will keep us from hurting others;
    which will keep us from shaming ourselves;
    which will keep us from being untrue to you.
Grant us that love of you,
    which will keep us from grieving your heart;
    which will keep us from frustrating your purposes;
    which will keep us from disappointing your hopes.
Grant us that love of you,
    which will make us love you,
      as you have first loved us;
    which will make us love our fellow men,
      as you have loved them;
    which will make us give ourselves for him,
      who loved us and gave himself for us.

So grant that,
  fearing you and loving you,
    we may be safe from sin,
    and strong in devotion;

      through Jesus Christ our Lord. Amen.

The Third Sunday after Trinity

O Lord, we beseech thee mercifully to hear us; and grant that we, to whom thou hast given an hearty desire to pray, may by thy mighty aid be defended and comforted in all dangers and adversities; through Jesus Christ our Lord. Amen.

Epistle: I Peter 5.5-11   *Gospel:* Luke 15.1-10

O God, our Father we thank you that you have put into our hearts the desire to pray. We thank you that you have made us such that in any time of trouble we instinctively turn to you.

We thank you that you have given us the gift of prayer,
    that your ear is ever listening
        to catch our every word,
           and to hear even the heart's unspoken cry for help;
    that the door to your presence
        is never shut,
           to him who seeks to enter on his knees.

We thank you that you have given us the confidence to pray. We thank you that you have told us,
    that you are our Father,
    that your name is love;
    that you love each one of us,
        as if there was only one of us to love,
           and that no child of yours can be lost in the crowd.

We thank you that you have given us
    unanswerable proof of your love,
        by sending your Son Jesus Christ,
            to live, to suffer and to die for us.

Give us now an answer to our prayers.
    We do not ask that we should be protected from all pain and sorrow, from all danger and distress. We ask for humility to accept whatever comes to us, and for courage, and fortitude and endurance to come safely through it, and to come out on the other side finer in character, and nearer to you.

    We do not ask that you should answer our prayers as we in our ignorance would wish, but as you in your mercy and love know best.

        Into your hands we commend our spirits,
            because we know that
                you are love to care,
                mercy to bless,
                power to save.

Hear these our prayers for your love's sake. Amen.

The Fourth Sunday after Trinity

O God, the protector of all that trust in thee, without whom nothing is strong, nothing is holy: Increase and multiply upon us thy mercy; that, thou being our ruler and guide, we may so pass through things temporal, that we finally lose not the things eternal: Grant this, O heavenly Father, for Jesus Christ's sake our Lord. Amen.

Epistle: Romans 8.18-23   *Gospel:* Luke 6.36-42

O God, you are our refuge and strength, and without you we can do nothing.

> Unless you strengthen us,
>> We cannot bear our burdens;
>> We cannot face our responsibilities;
>> We cannot stand the strain and the tension of life.

> Unless you guide us,
>> We cannot make the right decisions;
>> We cannot find the right way;
>> We cannot bring life in safety to its journey's end.

O God, our Father, you are the Holy One and the Source of all goodness and without you we cannot live aright.

> Unless you cleanse us,
>> We cannot conquer our temptations;
>> We cannot tame our passions;
>> We cannot master our desires.

Unless you control us,
We cannot guard our thoughts;
We cannot discipline our speech;
We cannot do only the things which are right.

O God, help us to submit to you, that you may strengthen us and guide us, that you may cleanse us and control us, that you may be our Ruler and our Guide, so that all through life we may walk in the way everlasting and finally enter without shame into your presence; through Jesus Christ our Lord. Amen.

The Fifth Sunday after Trinity

Grant, O Lord, we beseech thee, that the course of this world may be so peaceably ordered by thy governance, that thy Church may joyfully serve thee in all godly quietness; through Jesus Christ our Lord. Amen.

Epistle: I Peter 3.8-15   *Gospel:* Luke 5.1-11

O God, Ruler of all, grant that the state of the world may be such that everywhere doors may open for the truth of your word and the saving power of your gospel to spread unhindered throughout it.

Take from the world all threats of war. Enable the nations to live in brotherhood together. Teach men to direct the powers which you have given them not to the destroying but to the saving of life. Make men to know that this is one world, and that those who are in it must be one.

Take from the world all religious intolerance. Help all men to remember that there are more ways than one to you, and that you have your own secret stairway into every heart. Grant that we may not brand as heretics all who do not think as we do.

Take from the Church its divisions. Bring quickly the time when indeed there will be one flock and one shepherd. Help men to think far more of the Christ who unites, and far less of the systems which divide.

Take from all lands all enmity between class and class and party and party. Help all men to see beyond their individual interests to the common good.

Take from the world all enmity and suspicion between nation and nation, between race and race, between colour and colour. Help them to find a new fellowship which will transcend colour and country, and which will make them one family in you.

Take from the world all injustice and all poverty and make it a world where poverty shall cease to fester and where none shall prey on any other.

Hear these our prayers, and inspire us by your Spirit and strengthen us by your grace to build the kind of world this world ought to be through Jesus Christ our Lord. Amen.

The Sixth Sunday after Trinity

O God, who hast prepared for them that love thee such good things as pass man's understanding: Pour into our hearts such love toward thee, that we, loving thee above all things, may obtain thy promises, which exceed all that we can desire; through Jesus Christ our Lord. Amen.

Epistle: Romans 6.3-11   *Gospel:* Matthew 5.20-26

O God, our Father, you have loved us with an everlasting love, and in your mercy you have great rewards for those who are loyal to you. Help us so to live that we shall one day enter into these things which you have promised to your faithful servants.

Give us such a love of you,
    that we may find obedience,
        not a burden but a delight;
    that we may find the cost of loyalty,
        not a trial but a privilege;
    that we may find your law,
        not a chain to bind us,
        but wings to uplift us.

Give us such a love of our fellow men,
    that we may find service,
        not wearisome but joyous;
    that we may find giving,
        not a pain but a pleasure;
    that we may find sharing,
        not a duty but a joy.

Give us such a love of your Church,
  that we may find its worship,
    not a dead convention,
    but a living thrill;
  that we may find the obligations of church member-
  ship,
    not something to resent,
    but something in which to rejoice;
  that we may find work within it,
    not an imposition,
    but an opportunity.

So grant that love
  may sweeten all obedience,
  and lighten every task,

so that living for you, for our fellow men, and for your
Church may be all joy; through Jesus Christ our Lord.
Amen.

The Seventh Sunday after Trinity

Lord of all power and might, who art the author and giver of all good things: Graft in our hearts the love of thy Name, increase in us true religion, nourish us with all goodness, and of thy great mercy keep us in the same; through Jesus Christ our Lord. Amen.

Epistle: Romans 6.19-23   *Gospel:* Mark 8.1-10

O God, our Father, Giver of every good and perfect gift,

>Give us in our living true love of you.
>Give us the love,
>>which will grudge no gift,
>>which will refuse no obedience,
>>which will resent no trial.
>
>Give us in our living true religion.
>Help us,
>>to show our love for you
>>>by loving others;
>>to be in the world,
>>>and yet to keep our garments
>>>unspotted by the world;
>>to make the deeds of our hands
>>>match the words of our lips.
>
>Give us in our living true goodness.
>Give us the goodness,
>>which is not only pure,
>>>but also lovely;

which does not sin itself,
  but which loves the sinner;
which has upon it the reflection
  of the loveliness of the life of Jesus.

Give us in our living the gift of perseverance.
  When we have chosen our way,
    help us never to stray from it;
  when we fall,
    help us always to rise again;
  when there is a cross to bear,
    help us to see beyond it the crown.
So help us to live life
    in love, in service, and in fidelity,
    that we may come to the end in peace,
    and enter into blessedness;
        through Jesus Christ our Lord. Amen.

The Eighth Sunday after Trinity

O God, whose never-failing providence ordereth all things both in heaven and earth: We humbly beseech thee to put away from us all hurtful things, and to give us those things which be profitable for us; through Jesus Christ our Lord. Amen.

Epistle: Romans 8.12-17   *Gospel:* Matthew 7.15-21

O God, our Father, we know that the issues of life and death are in your hands, and we know that you are loving us with an everlasting love. If it is your will, grant to us to live in happiness and in peace.

> In all our undertakings,
>> Grant us prosperity and good success.

> In all our friendships,
>> Grant us to find our friends faithful and true

> In all bodily things,
>> Make us fit and healthy,
>>> Able for the work of the day.

> In all the things of the mind,
>> Make us calm and serene,
>>> Free from anxiety and worry.

> In material things,
>> Save us from poverty and from want.

> In spiritual things,
>> Save us from doubt and from distrust.

Grant us
    In our work satisfaction;
    In our study true wisdom;
    In our pleasure gladness;
    In our love loyalty.

And if misfortune does come to us, grant that any trial may only bring us closer to one another and closer to you; and grant that nothing may shake our certainty that you work all things together for good, and that a Father's hand will never cause his child a needless tear.

Hear this our prayer; through Jesus Christ our Lord. Amen.

The Ninth Sunday after Trinity

Grant to us, Lord, we beseech thee, the spirit to think and do always such things as be rightful; that we, who cannot do anything that is good without thee, may by thee be enabled to live according to thy will; through Jesus Christ our Lord. Amen.

Epistle: I Corinthians 10.1-13　　　　*Gospel:* Luke 16.1-9

O God, our Father, we know our own weakness and we know your power. And this day we take

> Our helplessness to your strength;
> Our ignorance to your wisdom;
> Our sin to your purity;
> Our need to your love.

We cannot decide aright what we should do;
> Grant us the guidance which will save us from all mistakes.

We cannot conquer our temptations;
> Grant us the grace which can make us clean and keep us clean.

We cannot bear the toil of life;
> Grant us the strength to pass the breaking-point and not to break.

We cannot escape the worry of life;
> Grant us the peace that passes understanding,
> which the world cannot give or ever take away.

106

We cannot face the responsibilities of life;
> Grant us to know that there is nothing that we have to
> face alone.

We cannot solve the problems of life;
> Grant us in your wisdom to find the answers
> to the questions which perplex our ignorance.

We cannot find the right way;
> Grant that at every cross-roads of life
> your Spirit may be there to direct us.

We cannot face life alone;
> Grant us to remember that our Lord is with us always
> to the end of the world and beyond.

We cannot face death alone;
> Grant us to be very sure that nothing in life or in death,
> can separate us from your love in Christ Jesus our
> Lord.

We come to you for strength in life and for hope when life is ended; through Jesus Christ our Lord. Amen.

The Tenth Sunday after Trinity

Let thy merciful ears, O Lord, be open to the prayers of thy humble servants; and that they may obtain their petitions make them to ask such things as shall please thee; through Jesus Christ our Lord. Amen.

Epistle: I Corinthians 12.1-11   *Gospel:* Luke 19.41-47a

O God, our Father, help us only to desire in our hearts and only to ask in our prayers the things which please you.

Help us to ask that we may learn,
  not how to get our own way,
    but how to take your way;
  not how to do what we want,
    but how to do what you want.

Help us to ask that we may learn,
  not how to grow rich in this world's goods,
    but how to lay up treasure in heaven;
  not how to realize our dreams of worldly greatness
    but how to live in humble service.

Help us to ask that we may learn,
  not how to live in the independence of pride,
    but in dependence on you;
  not how to know and plan the future,
    but how to take one step at a time,
      our hand in yours.

Help us to ask that we may learn,
   not how to gratify,
     but how to master our desires;
   not how to satisfy,
     but how to tame our passions.

Help us to ask that we may learn,
   not how to live as if this world were all,
     but how to live
     as pilgrims of eternity,
     who have here no abiding city,
     but who are on the way to that city,
     whose maker and builder you are;
   not how to please ourselves in this world,
     but how to meet your judgment,
     when this world is ended.

Hear these our prayers; through Jesus Christ our Lord.
Amen.

The Eleventh Sunday after Trinity

O God, who declarest thy almighty power most chiefly in shewing mercy and pity: Mercifully grant unto us such a measure of thy grace, that we, running the way of thy commandments, may obtain thy gracious promises, and be made partakers of thy heavenly treasure; through Jesus Christ our Lord. Amen.

Epistle: I Corinthians 15.1-11   *Gospel:* Luke 18.9-14

O God, our Father, we come to you,

> Not because we are strong,
> but because we are weak;
> Not because we have any merits of our own,
> but because we need mercy and help.

Grant unto us this day the mercy and the pity which are yours.

Give us grace,

> Always to keep your commandments;
> Always to accept your guidance;
> Always to obey your word;
> Never to leave your path,
> but always to walk in the way everlasting.

Give us grace,

> So to run,
> > that we may reach our goal;

So to fight,
    that we may win the victor's crown;
So to keep the faith,
    that to the very end we may be true.

Give us grace so to live in time that we may receive the true treasure in eternity.

Help us to be,
    So pure in heart,
      that we may see you;
    So faithful unto death,
      that we may receive the crown of life;
    So close to you in our walk upon earth,
      that, when earth is ended,
        we may be for ever with our Lord.

In your mercy and pity,

    Make our ignorance wise with your wisdom;
    Make our weakness strong with your strength,
      so that our brief life may be clothed with your eternal
      life;
        through Jesus Christ our Lord. Amen.

Almighty and everlasting God, who art always more ready to hear than we to pray, and art wont to give more than either we desire, or deserve: Pour down upon us the abundance of thy mercy; forgiving us those things whereof our conscience is afraid, and giving us those good things which we are not worthy to ask, but through the merits and mediation of Jesus Christ, thy Son, our Lord. Amen.

Epistle: II Corinthians 3.4-9   *Gospel:* Mark 7.31-37

O God, our Father, we cannot doubt your generous love. We know that, if you gave us the gift of your Son, you will with him freely give us all things.

We know that, even when we sin, you still love us, and your only desire is that we should repent and come back to you. Forgive us for our sins.

> For the things which we try to hide from others;
> For the things which we try to put out of our minds and forget;
> For the things for which others find it very difficult to forgive us;
> For the things for which we cannot forgive ourselves;
> For the things which sometimes in our folly we try to hide from you:
> > Forgive us, O God.

112

For the heartbreak and the sorrow, the worry and the anxiety we have caused;

For any time when we made it easier for some one else to go wrong;

For the harm that we have done, and can never now undo:

> Forgive us, O God.

Grant us the gifts which you alone can give.

Give us,
> The courage to admit our mistakes;
> The grace which will enable us to rise when we fall, and to begin all over again when we fail;
> The real penitence, which humbly and sincerely asks for forgiveness, when it has done wrong.

Give us this day,
> Forgiveness for the past;
> Courage for the present;
> Hope for the future,

And in your infinite mercy come to meet our infinite need; through Jesus Christ our Lord. Amen.

The Thirteenth Sunday after Trinity

Almighty and merciful God, of whose only gift it cometh that thy faithful people do unto thee true and laudable service: Grant, we beseech thee, that we may so faithfully serve thee in this life, that we fail not finally to attain thy heavenly promises; through the merits of Jesus Christ our Lord. Amen.

Epistle: Galatians 3.16-22   *Gospel:* Luke 10.23-37

Eternal God, we know that in our own strength we cannot give you the service that we ought to give. So then we ask you to give us what we need to enable us to serve you more nearly as we ought.

Give us
  Self-discipline,
    so that we may choose,
    not what we wish but what we ought;

  Strength of will,
    so that we may accept the right,
      however difficult it is,
    and refuse the wrong,
      however attractive it is;

  Obedience,
    so that in doing your will
    we may find our peace;

Trust,
    so that we may be able willingly to accept
      even that which we do not understand,
    and so that, whatever happens,
      we may never doubt your love.

In every time of decision,
    give us light to see what we ought to do,
      and give us resolution, courage and strength to
        do it;

In every time of temptation,
    give us strength to resist all evil,
      and to do the right;

In every time of effort,
    give us power to do what by ourselves we could
    not do,
      and perseverance to bring the task to its ap-
      pointed end;

In every time of sorrow,
    give us grace to remember
    that we have hopes as well as memories,
    so that we may think more of the glory of life
      eternal,
    than of the brief darkness of death.

So grant that guided and strengthened by you
    we may live in honour,
    and come to the end in peace,
    and finally enter into glory;

through Jesus Christ our Lord. Amen.

The Fourteenth Sunday after Trinity

Almighty and everlasting God, give unto us the increase of faith, hope, and charity; and, that we may obtain that which thou dost promise, make us to love that which thou dost command; through Jesus Christ our Lord. Amen.

Epistle: Galatians 5.16-24   *Gospel:* Luke 17.11-19

O God, our Father, you alone can enable us to accept and to obey your commandments and to do your will.

Increase our faith.
>   Help us,
>>   To trust you when the skies are dark;
>>   To accept that which we cannot understand;
>>   To be quite sure that all things can work together for good to those who love you.

Increase our hope.
>   Give us
>>   The hope which has seen things at their worst,
>>   and which refuses to despair;
>>   The hope that is able to fail,
>>   and yet to try again;
>>   The hope which can accept disappointment,
>>   and yet not abandon hope.

Increase our love.
>   Help us,
>>   To love our fellow men as you love them;
>>   To love you as you have first loved us;
>>   To love loyalty to our Lord above all other things.

116

Help us so to love you that your commandments will never be a weariness and a burden to us, but that it will be a joy for us to obey them, so that in obedience to you we may find our perfect freedom, and in doing your will our peace.

So grant to us,
> To fight the good fight;
> To run the straight race;
> To keep the faith,
>> that we may win the glory and the crown.

Hear these our prayers for your love's sake. Amen.

The Fifteenth Sunday after Trinity

Keep, we beseech thee, O Lord, thy Church with thy perpetual mercy; and, because the frailty of man without thee cannot but fall, keep us ever by thy help from all things hurtful, and lead us to all things profitable to our salvation; through Jesus Christ our Lord. Amen.

Epistle: Galatians 6.11-18   *Gospel:* Matthew 6.24-34

O God, our Father, we know our own weakness.

> Our minds are darkened,
>> and by ourselves we cannot find and know the truth.
>
> Our wills are weak,
>> and by ourselves we cannot resist temptation,
>> or bring to its completion that which we resolve to do.
>
> Our hearts are fickle,
>> and by ourselves we cannot give to you
>> the loyalty which is your due.
>
> Our steps are faltering,
>> and by ourselves we cannot walk in your straight way.

So this day we ask you,

> To enlighten us;
> To strengthen us;
> To guide us,

that we may know you, and love you, and follow you all the days of our life.

Give to your Church your blessing and your protection.

Guide her in her thinking,
   that she may be saved from the heresies
   which destroy the faith.

Strengthen her in her witness,
   that she may bring no discredit on the name she
   bears.

Inspire her in her fellowship,
   that those who enter her may find within her
   your friendship and the friendship of their fellow
   men.

So grant that guided, strengthened, and inspired by you, your Church may shine like a beacon of truth, of loyalty, and of love within the darkness of the world; through Jesus Christ our Lord. Amen.

The Sixteenth Sunday after Trinity

O Lord, we beseech thee, let thy continual pity cleanse and defend thy Church; and, because it cannot continue in safety without thy succour, preserve it evermore by thy help and goodness; through Jesus Christ our Lord. Amen.

Epistle: Ephesians 3.13-21   *Gospel:* Luke 7.11-17

O God, our Father, you intended the Church to be the Body of Jesus Christ, your Son. You meant the Church to be a voice to speak for him, hands to work for him, feet to go upon his errands; and without your help the Church can never be what you meant it to be.

We ask you to cleanse the Church.
>   All bitterness that would disturb its fellowship;
>   All divisions that would destroy its unity;
>   All coldness that would lessen its devotion;
>   All slackness that would paralyse its action:
>   Take from your Church, O God.

We ask you to defend the Church.
>   From all persecution and attack from without;
>   From all heresy and false doctrine from within;
>   From the hostility of its enemies and the failure of its members:
>   Defend your Church, O God.

We ask you to help and to assist your Church.
Give to it
>   Courage in its speaking,
>   And tirelessness in its acting.

Give to it
> Ministers who are men,
> In whose minds there is true learning,
> On whose lips there is eloquence,
> In whose hearts there is devotion,
> Who are men apt to study, skilled to teach,
> Wise to counsel, brave to act, loving to help.

Give to it
> Members who are generous in giving, faithful in prayer,
> Diligent in worship, Christlike in witness.

So grant that, preserved by your help and goodness, the Church may indeed be the Body of Jesus Christ. This we ask for your love's sake. Amen.

The Seventeenth Sunday after Trinity

Lord, we pray thee that thy grace may always prevent and follow us, and make us continually to be given to all good works; through Jesus Christ our Lord. Amen.

Epistle: Ephesians 4.1-6   *Gospel:* Luke 14.1-11

O God, our Father, we know that your grace is sufficient for all things. Give to us at all times this all-sufficient grace, that in it our weakness may be made strong, our ignorance wise, and our sins forgiven.

>Let your grace go ever before us,
>>That we may know the way to take;
>>That we may see the path in which we ought to walk;
>>That at each cross-roads of life
>>>we may see the road we ought to choose;
>>That without falling and without straying
>>>we may in safety reach our journey's end.

>Let your grace follow after us,
>>That we may ever be
>>>Protected by your power,
>>>Upheld by your kindness,
>>>Warmed by your love.

So equip us with your grace that men may see our good works and glorify you our Father in Heaven.

>By your grace make us
>>Firm in resolution,
>>Courageous in action,
>>Constant in devotion,

Unwearying in forgiveness,
Loyal in love,
Lovely in life.

So grant that guided and protected, upheld and equipped by your grace we may live

To our own honour,
In the service of our fellow men,
And to your glory.

This we ask through Jesus Christ our Lord. Amen.

The Eighteenth Sunday after Trinity

Lord, we beseech thee, grant thy people grace to withstand the temptations of the world, the flesh, and the devil, and with pure hearts and minds to follow thee the only God; through Jesus Christ our Lord. Amen.

Epistle: I Corinthians 1.4-8   *Gospel:* Matthew 22.34-46

O God, our Father, because we are men and women with human hearts and human minds and human emotions, there is no escape for us from temptation.

Defend us from the temptations of the world.
From lowering our standards and abandoning our ideals;
From the cautious conformity that fears to be different;
From the materialism which really believes that a man's life does consist in the abundance of the things he possesses:
Defend us, O God.

Defend us from the temptations of the flesh.
From the passion which can wreck life;
From the impulses which can bring regret to follow;
From the too strong emotions which can sweep us to disaster;
From the freedom which has become licence and the love which has become lust:
Defend us, O God.

Defend us from the temptations of the devil.
> From yielding to any seduction to sin;
> From the power of the fascination of the forbidden thing;
> From forgetting that in the end our sin
>> is bound to find us out:
>>> Defend us, O God.

Give us by your grace
> Hearts so pure that they love only the highest;
> Minds so clean that they seek only the truth.

And grant that nothing may lure us from our loyalty, and nothing deflect us from our path; and so help us all our days ever to follow you and never to turn back and never to lose our way: through Jesus Christ our Lord. Amen.

O God, forasmuch as without thee we are not able to please thee: Mercifully grant that thy Holy Spirit may in all things direct and rule our hearts; through Jesus Christ our Lord. Amen.

Epistle: Ephesians 4.17-32   *Gospel:* Matthew 9.1-8

O God, our Father, we are helpless without your help.

> Unless you help us,
>> we can see the ideal,
>>> but we cannot reach it;
>> we can know the right,
>>> but we cannot do it;
>> we can recognize our duty,
>>> but we cannot perform it;
>> we can seek the truth,
>>> but we can never wholly find it.

All our lives we are haunted by the difference between what we ought to do and what in fact we can do.

> By your Holy Spirit,
>> Enlighten our minds,
>>> that we may reach beyond guessing to knowing,
>>> and beyond doubting to certainty.
>> Purify our hearts,
>>> that the wrong desires may not only be kept under control,
>>> but may be completely taken away.

126

Strengthen our wills,
    that we may pass beyond resolving to doing,
    and beyond intention to action.

By your Holy Spirit,
    Break for us the habits we cannot break;
    Conquer for us the fears we cannot conquer;
    Calm for us the worries we cannot still;
    Soothe for us the sorrows no human comfort can ease;
    Answer for us the questions no human wisdom can answer.

O God, our Father, this day we rest our weakness in your strength, and our insufficiency in your completeness. Take us, and do for us what we cannot do, and make us what we cannot be; through Jesus Christ our Lord. Amen.

The Twentieth Sunday after Trinity

*O almighty and most merciful God, of thy bountiful good-
ness keep us, we beseech thee, from all things that may
hurt us; that we, being ready both in body and soul, may
cheerfully accomplish those things that thou wouldest have
done; through Jesus Christ our Lord.* Amen.

Epistle: Ephesians 5.15-21   *Gospel:* Matthew 22.1-14

O God, our Father, protect us from all that would hurt us
in body, mind, or spirit.

Protect us from all that would injure our bodies.
> From habits which would injure our health;
> From the greed or the self-indulgence which would
> leave us soft and flabby;
> From any practice that would make our body a less
> efficient servant of our mind:
>> Protect us, O God.

Protect us from all would injure our minds.
> From the mental laziness that will not think;
> From that preoccupation with cheap and trivial things
> which saps the ability of the mind to deal with the
> things which really matter;
> From the prejudice which blinds us to the truth and
> which makes us misjudge other people:
>> Protect us, O God.

Protect us from all that would injure our hearts.
>From the pride that separates us from you;
>From the self-righteousness which separates us from
our fellow men;
>From the self-will that will listen to no other voice,
human or divine, than the voice of its own desires;
Protect us, O God.

And so grant that by your protection being
strong in body;
vigorous in mind;
pure in spirit,

we may be enabled to do the work which you need us to do:
through Jesus Christ our Lord. Amen.

The Twenty-first Sunday after Trinity

Grant, we beseech thee, merciful Lord to thy faithful people pardon and peace, that they may be cleansed from all their sins, and serve thee with a quiet mind; through Jesus Christ our Lord. Amen.

Epistle: Ephesians 6.10-20   *Gospel:* John 4.46b-54

O God, our Father, lover of the souls of men, grant us today your pardon and your peace.

> For the sins of our lips;
>> For words untrue and words unclean and words unkind;
> For the sins of our hands;
>> For all careless work, for all wrong deeds,
>>> for any action which hurt another,
>>>> or which it made it easier for him to go wrong;
> For the sins of our minds;
>> For blindness to the truth, for refusal to face the facts,
>>> for all dishonest thinking;
> For the sins of our hearts;
>> For all pride, all wrong desires,
>>> and all false loves:
>>>> Forgive us, O God.

Grant us this day, O God,
> Peace within ourselves,
>> that our inner tensions may be taken away;

that we may no longer be torn in indecision;
that we may no longer be for ever halting between
two opinions.

Grant us this day, O God,
Peace with our fellow men,
that we may not disturb the fellowship by disputing;
that we may never quarrel within our homes or outside them;
that we may live in unity with all.

Grant us this day, O God,
Peace with you,
that the certainty that you love us
may take all fear away;
that we may know,
that your love has forgiven us;
that your grace upholds us;
that your welcome awaits us.

And so grant that we may live at peace with ourselves, in
fellowship with our fellow men, and at one with you;
through Jesus Christ our Lord. Amen.

Lord, we beseech thee to keep thy household the Church in continual godliness; that through thy protection it may be free from all adversities, and devoutly given to serve thee in good works, to the glory of thy Name; through Jesus Christ our Lord. Amen.

Epistle: Philippians 1.3-11   *Gospel:* Matthew 18.21-35

O God, our Father, bless your Church.

Help us always to remember that the Church is your family;

And so help us within the Church never to do anything to grieve your fatherly heart,

And never to do anything to turn to bitterness the brotherly love, which ought to be the very air and atmosphere of your Church.

Give your Church grace to live in all godliness.

In this generation give your Church grace to be,
adventurous in thought and resolute in action;
courageous in witness and generous in service.

In this generation give your Church grace to have,
wisdom in its mind, certainty in its message;
love in its fellowship and a passionate desire to win those who are still outside.

Keep your Church free from persecution from outside and from dissension inside.

Strengthen your Church within the world that it may stand
   Like a stedfast rock
      amid the shifting sands
         of doubt and unbelief;
   Like a clear light of goodness
      amid the falling of standards,
         and the lowering of ideals;
   Like a warm fire of love
      amid the coldness of selfishness
         and the callousness of self-seeking.

So help your Church,
   To accept nothing but your guidance;
   To serve nothing but your will;
   To seek nothing but your glory;

through Jesus Christ our Lord. Amen.

The Twenty-third Sunday after Trinity

O God, our refuge and strength, who art the author of all godliness: Be ready we beseech thee, to hear the devout prayers of thy Church; and grant that those things which we ask faithfully we may obtain effectually; through Jesus Christ our Lord. Amen.

Epistle: Philippians 3.17-21   *Gospel:* Matthew 22.15-22

O God, you are our refuge.

> When we are exhausted by life's efforts;
> When we are bewildered by life's problems;
> When we are wounded by life's sorrows:
>> We come for refuge to you.

O God, you are our strength.

> When our tasks are beyond our powers;
> When our temptations are too strong for us;
> When duty calls for more than we have to give to it:
>> We come for strength to you.

O God, it is from you that all goodness comes.

> It is from you that our ideals come;
> It is from you that there comes to us
>> the spur of high desire and the restraint of conscience.
> It is from you that there has come the strength
>> to resist any temptation,
>> and to do any good thing.

134

And now as we pray to you,

> Help us to believe in your love,
>   so that we may be certain
>   that you will hear our prayer;

> Help us to believe in your power,
>   so that we may be certain
>   that you are able to do for us
>   above all that we ask or think;

> Help us to believe in your wisdom,
>   so that we may be certain
>   that you will answer,
>   not as our ignorance asks,
>   but as your perfect wisdom knows best.

All this we ask through Jesus Christ our Lord. Amen.

O Lord, we beseech thee, absolve thy people from their offences; that through thy bountiful goodness we may all be delivered from the bands of those sins, which by our frailty we have committed: Grant this, O heavenly Father, for Jesus Christ's sake, our blessed Lord and Saviour. Amen.

Epistle: Colossians 1.3-12   *Gospel:* Matthew 9.18-26

O God, our Father, you know us better than we know ourselves, and you know our weakness and our frailty.

Our minds are too easily led.
Too often we are too easily influenced
by specious arguments,
which seek to prove what we would like to be true.

Our hearts are too easily swayed.
Too often we are fickle and inconstant in our devotion,
and so the fascination of the false love
lures us from the true.

Our memories are too forgetful.
We forget what we have learned;
We forget the experiences,
which should have been a lasting warning to us;
We forget the gratitude we ought ever to remember.

Our wills are too weak.
We can resolve, but we cannot do;
We can know, but we cannot obey;
We can decide, but we cannot carry out.

So by our continual sinning we have become the slaves of sin.

> There are things we do, not because we want to do them, but because we cannot help doing them.
>
> There are habits which we long to break, and cannot break.
>
> There are things we do, because, although we know they are wrong, we cannot stop ourselves.

O God, forgive us for all past sin. Break by your power the chains that bind us; and in the future so let your recreating power remake us that for us also the old things may pass away and all things may become new; through Jesus Christ our Lord. Amen.

The Twenty-fifth Sunday after Trinity

Stir up, we beseech thee, O Lord, the wills of thy faithful people; that they, plenteously bringing forth the fruit of good works, may of thee be plenteously rewarded; through Jesus Christ our Lord. Amen.

Lesson: Jeremiah 23.5-8   *Gospel:* John 6.5-14

O God, our Father, strengthen our wills this day.

> Clear sight, that we may recognize the things that matter and the things that do not matter;
> A sense of proportion, that we may see which things are worth getting excited about, and which things are not important;
> Wisdom, that in all life's choices we may be enabled to choose aright:
>> Grant us these things, O God.

> Independence, that popularity or unpopularity may not affect our decisions;
> Perseverance, that, having begun a good thing, we may not lay it down until we have completed it;
> Determination, that nothing may deflect us from our chosen way:
>> Grant us these things, O God.

O God, our Father, by your grace make us fruitful in all good works.

> Kindness, that no one in need may ever appeal to us in vain;

Generosity, that we may be concerned, not with how little, but with how much we can give;

Loyalty, that, though all men deny you, we may still be true;

Love, that like our Master we may be among our fellow men as those who serve:
    Grant us these things, O God.

O God, our Father, grant us at the end to enter into our reward.

    Help us to live so close to our blessed Lord
        That death may be only an entering into his nearer presence;
        That we may so live that even here and now we may know the life which is eternal;
        That we may so live each day that at the end of all days we may hear you say, Well done!

Hear these our prayers; through Jesus Christ our Lord. Amen.

Saint Andrew's Day

Almighty God, who didst give such grace unto thy Holy Apostle Saint Andrew, that he readily obeyed the calling of thy Son Jesus Christ, and followed him without delay: Grant unto us all, that we, being called by thy holy Word, may forthwith give up ourselves obediently to fulfil thy holy commandments; through the same Jesus Christ our Lord. Amen.

Epistle: Romans 10.9-21   *Gospel:* Matthew 4.18-22

O Lord Jesus, help us to accept your call as Andrew did.

Help us, as Andrew did, to hear your call above the many voices of the world.

Grant that
> the claims of business;
> the attractions of pleasure;
> the cares of this world

may not make us fail to hear your call.

Help us, as Andrew did, to obey at once; and grant that we may not put off until tomorrow that decision which we ought to make today.

Help us, as Andrew did, to give ourselves wholly to your obedience.

Cleanse us from
> the self-will, which would make us want nothing but our own way;
> the lack of discipline, which would make us refuse to make the effort which obedience demands;

the subjection to the fear, or the desire for the favour, of men, which would make us refuse your commandments;

the love of comfort and security, which would make us take the easy rather than the right way.

Help us here and now to accept your call, that one day we may share your glory. This we ask for your love's sake. Amen.

Saint Andrew's Day is 30*th November.*

Saint Thomas the Apostle

Almighty and everlasting God, who for the more confirmation of the faith didst suffer thy holy Apostle Thomas to be doubtful in thy Son's resurrection: Grant us so perfectly and without all doubt, to believe in thy Son Jesus Christ, that our faith in thy sight may never be reproved. Hear us, O Lord, through the same Jesus Christ, to whom with thee and the Holy Ghost, be all honour and glory, now and for evermore. Amen.

Epistle: Ephesians 2.19-22   *Gospel:* John 20.24-31

O God, our Father, it encourages us to know that even an Apostle lost and found his faith.

There is so much in this life to take our faith away:
> The problems to which there is no solution;
> The questions to which there is no answer;
> The sorrows for which there is no comfort;
> The tears of things for which there is no consolation;
> The pains for which there is no cure;
> The tragedies for which there is no explanation.

> Sometimes even the door of prayer seems shut;
> Sometimes the burden of life and the mystery of death overwhelm us;
> Sometimes we feel that there is no fidelity in man and no answer from you.

> Sometimes we feel battered and buffeted by the storm of life;

142

Sometimes our minds are bewildered and our hearts are broken.

At times like that help us to remember Thomas who lost and found his faith again.

Help us to remember our blessed Lord who on his Cross cried out: 'My God, my God, why have you forsaken me?' And help us like him to hold on until the dark changes to the dawn again, and we can say in perfect faith, made stronger by the testing, 'Father, into your hands I commend my spirit.'

Hear this our prayer; through Jesus Christ our Lord. Amen.

Saint Thomas's Day is 21*st December.*

The Conversion of Saint Paul

O God, who, through the preaching of the blessed Apostle Saint Paul, hast caused the light of the Gospel to shine throughout the world: Grant, we beseech thee, that we, having his wonderful conversion in remembrance, may show forth our thankfulness unto thee for the same, by following the holy doctrine which he taught; through Jesus Christ our Lord. Amen.

Lesson: Acts 9.1-22   *Gospel:* Matthew 19.27-30

O God, today we thank you for Paul, the apostle to the Gentiles, the apostle to us.

We thank you for the grace which changed him
from the persecutor to the servant of the faith;
Help us also so to love you and so to surrender to you,
that we too may find the grace
which makes all things new.

We thank you for his skill and wisdom
in argument and in debate, in preaching and in writing,
through which many in many lands were brought to Jesus Christ;
Help us to take every talent and every gift which we possess,
and to lay them on the altar of your service,
that we too may be used to bring others to you.

144

We thank you for the courage and the endurance
  with which he travelled over land and sea
    to preach the gospel;
Help us to be ready to give, and even to sacrifice,
  our time, our energy, our money,
    to help and serve your Church wherever we live.

We thank you for the way in which he faced
  slander and persecution, imprisonment, trial and
  death.
Help us also, if need be,
  to suffer rather than to be false to the faith.

We thank you for the gospel
  which he preached to men;
Help us also so to live
  that by the wisdom of our words and the power of
  our example,
    others may be moved to give their hearts to you.

This we ask through Jesus Christ our Lord. Amen.

The date of the Conversion of Saint Paul is 25th January.

The Presentation of Christ in the Temple, commonly called, The Purification of Saint Mary the Virgin

Almighty and everliving God, we humbly beseech thy Majesty, that, as thy only-begotten Son was this day presented in the temple in substance of our flesh, so we may be presented unto thee with pure and clean hearts, by the same thy Son Jesus Christ our Lord. Amen.

Lesson: Malachi 3.1-5   *Gospel:* Luke 2.22-40

O God, we remember how this day our blessed Lord was presented as a little baby in the Temple in Jerusalem. Grant that even so we may present ourselves as an offering to you.

Help us to offer our bodies to you,
    that we may live in purity and in chastity
        all the days of our life.

Help us to offer our minds to you,
    that all our thoughts may be pure and clean,
    that we may ever seek the truth,
        and never be satisfied with any false thing;
    that we may think with that utter honesty,
        which never evades the facts.

Help us to offer our hands to you,
    that you may enable us to use them
        in usefulness,
        to earn a living for ourselves and for those we love;
        in kindness,
        to help those who are in need of help;
        in gentleness,
        to soothe and to heal another's sorrow and pain.

Help us to offer our voices to you,
    that you may use us as heralds of your grace,
    and that through us comfort and courage
      may be brought to those who need them.

Help us to give our hearts to you,
    that we may so love you,
    that we may seek nothing but to please you,
    and fear nothing but to grieve you.

So help us to give back to you the life we owe, offering ourselves to you, body, soul and spirit, that in your service we may find our freedom and our peace and our life; through Jesus Christ our Lord. Amen.

The date of the Purification is 2nd February.

Saint Matthias's Day

O Almighty God, who into the place of the traitor Judas didst choose thy faithful servant Matthias to be of the number of the twelve Apostles: Grant that thy Church, being always preserved from false Apostles, may be ordered and guided by faithful and true pastors; through Jesus Christ our Lord. Amen.

Lesson: Acts 1.15-26   *Gospel:* Matthew 11.25-30

O God, you are the fountain of all truth; we ask you to protect your Church from all false teaching.

    Protect the Church
        From all teaching and preaching which would destroy men's faith;
        From all that removes the old foundations
            without putting anything in their place;
        From all that confuses the simple,
            that perplexes the seeker,
            that bewilders the way-faring man.

    And yet at the same time protect the Church
        From the failure to face new truth;
        From devotion to words and ideas
            which the passing of the years has rendered unintelligible;
        From all intellectual cowardice
            and from all mental lethargy and sloth.

O God, send to your Church teachers,
  Whose minds are wise with wisdom;
  Whose hearts are warm with love;
  Whose lips are eloquent with truth.

Send to your Church teachers
  Whose desire is to build and not to destroy;
  Who are adventurous with the wise,
    and yet gentle with the simple;
  Who strenuously exercise the intellect,
    and who yet remember that the heart has reasons
    of its own.

Give to your Church preachers and teachers who can make
known the Lord Christ to others because they know him
themselves; and give to your Church hearers, who, being
freed from prejudice, will follow truth as blind men long for
light. This we ask through Jesus Christ our Lord. Amen.

Saint Matthias's Day is 24th February.

The Annunciation of the blessed Virgin Mary

*We beseech thee, O Lord, pour thy grace into our hearts;
that, as we have known the incarnation of thy Son Jesus
Christ by the message of an angel, so by his cross and passion we may be brought unto the glory of his resurrection;
through the same Jesus Christ our Lord.* Amen.

Lesson: Isaiah 7.10-15   *Gospel:* Luke 1.26-38

O God, Father of your Son our Saviour Jesus Christ, help
us to know Jesus

> in his incarnation;
> in his cross and death;
> in his resurrection and his risen power.

Help us to know him in his incarnation.

> Help us to remember,
> That he grew up, as we must grow up;
> That he learned in obedience, as we have to learn;
> That he worked for a living, as we have to work;
> That he was tempted, as we are tempted;
> That he knew
> > the failure of love,
> > the malice of enemies,
> > the faithfulness of friends;
>
> That he was
> > the helper of all in need,
> > the healer of the sick,
> > the feeder of the hungry,

150

the comforter of the sad,
the friend of those who had no friends,
and whom all men despised.

Help us to know him in his death.

Help us to remember,
That he loved us and gave himself for us;
That he was obedient unto death;
That he gave his life a ransom for many,
a ransom for us.

Help us to know him in his resurrection and in his risen power.

Help us to remember,
That he conquered death,
and that he is alive for evermore;
That he is with us always,
to the end of time and beyond.

So help us to know our Lord in the beauty of his life, in the wonder of his death and in the power of his resurrection. This we ask for your love's sake. Amen.

The date of the Annunciation is 25th March.

Saint Mark's Day

O Almighty God, who hast instructed thy holy Church with the heavenly doctrine of thy Evangelist Saint Mark: Give us grace, that, being not like children carried away with every blast of vain doctrine, we may be established in the truth of thy holy Gospel; through Jesus Christ our Lord. Amen.

Epistle: Ephesians 4.7-16   *Gospel:* John 15.1-11

O God, we thank you for all those in whose words and in whose writings your truth has come to us.

> For the historians, the psalmists and the prophets,
>> who wrote the Old Testament;
> For those who wrote the Gospels and the Letters
>> of the New Testament;
> For all who in every generation
>> have taught and explained and expounded and preached
>>> the word of Scripture:
>>>> We thank you, O God.

Grant, O God, that no false teaching may ever have any power to deceive us or to seduce us from the truth.

> Grant, O God, that we may never listen to any teaching
>> which would encourage us to think
>>> sin less serious, vice more attractive,
>>>> or virtue less important;

Grant, O God, that we may never listen to any teaching which would dethrone Jesus Christ from the topmost place;

Grant, O God, that we may never listen to any teaching which for its own purposes perverts the truth.

O God, our Father, establish us immovably in the truth.

Give us minds which can see at once
the difference between the true and the false;

Make us able to test everything,
and to hold fast to that which is good;

Give us such a love of truth,
that no false thing may ever be able to lure us from it.

So grant that all our lives we may know, and love, and live the truth; through Jesus Christ our Lord. Amen.

Saint Mark's Day is 25th April.

Saint Philip and Saint James's Day

O Almighty God, whom truly to know is everlasting life: Grant us perfectly to know thy Son Jesus Christ to be the way, the truth, and the life; that, following the steps of thy holy Apostles, Saint Philip and Saint James, we may stedfastly walk in the way that leadeth to eternal life; through the same thy Son Jesus Christ our Lord. Amen.

Epistle: James 1.1-12   *Gospel:* John 14.1-13

O God, our Father, we remember that Jesus said: I am the way, the truth, and the life.

Help us to find in Jesus
    The way that leads from earth to heaven;
    The way that leads from time to eternity;
    The way that leads from the things that are visible
        to the things that are invisible;
    The way that leads to you.

Help us to find in Jesus
    The truth about ourselves,
        so that we may see both what we are
            and what we were meant to be;
    The truth about life that we may know
        that the way to gain life
            is to spend life,
        that the cross
            is the way to the crown;
    The truth about you,
        so that we may know that in Jesus
            we see exactly what you are like.

Help us to find in Jesus
>The life that is real life;
>The life that even on earth is a foretaste of heaven;
>The life that is your life;
>The life that not even death can extinguish.

And grant that we may ever walk the way your great apostles walked, so that with them we may enter into life eternal; through Jesus Christ our Lord. Amen.

St Philip and St James's Day is 1st May.

Saint Barnabas the Apostle

O Lord God Almighty, who didst endue thy Holy Apostle Barnabas with singular gifts of the Holy Ghost: Leave us not, we beseech thee, destitute of thy manifold gifts, nor yet of grace to use them alway to thy honour and glory; through Jesus Christ our Lord. Amen.

Lesson: Acts 11.22-30   *Gospel:* John 15.12-16

Let us think of the life of Barnabas and let us pray that our lives may become like his.

Let us think of Barnabas as the son of consolation (Acts 4.36).

Help us, O God, like Barnabas ever to be a comfort to the sad, a friend to the lonely and a consolation to the broken-hearted.

Let us think of Barnabas giving up his possessions (Acts 4.37).

Help us, O God, like Barnabas to take all that we have and to use it in your service and in the service of our fellow men, and help us to remember that giving is always better than getting.

Let us think of Barnabas standing guarantor for Paul (Acts 9.27).

O God, our Father, help us like Barnabas to stand by any man who is trying to live a new life; and help us never to condemn a man because of his past, but always to help every man who is making a new beginning.

156

Let us think of Barnabas sent to preach to the Gentiles (Acts 13.1).

O God, our Father, help us like Barnabas ever to desire to tell the story of Jesus to those who have not heard it; and, if we cannot ourselves go to other lands, make us to help the work by the offering of our prayers and the giving of our money; and make us to remember that there are many in our own country and in our own circle who have still to be brought to you.

Let us think of Barnabas with Paul in Lystra (Acts 14.12-20).

Help us, O God like Barnabas to witness for you even if it is difficult or dangerous to do so. So help us never to be ashamed of the gospel of Christ.

Give us, as you gave to Barnabas, the gifts we need to serve you in our time, and give us grace to use them; through Jesus Christ our Lord. Amen.

Saint Barnabas's Day is 11*th June.*

Saint John Baptist's Day

Almighty God, by whose providence thy servant John Baptist was wonderfully born, and sent to prepare the way of thy Son our Saviour, by preaching of repentance: Make us so to follow his doctrine and holy life, that we may truly repent according to his preaching; and after his example constantly speak the truth, boldly rebuke vice, and patiently suffer for the truth's sake; through Jesus Christ our Lord. Amen.

Lesson: Isaiah 40.1-11   *Gospel:* Luke 1.57-80

O God, our Father, help us in everything to follow the example of your servant John the Baptist.

Help us sincerely to repent.
> Show us the ugliness and the evil of our lives;
> Show us the harm we have done,
>> and the heartbreak that we have caused;
>
> Show us how we have shamed ourselves, disappointed those who love us, and grieved you.
> Make us truly sorry for all our sins and our mistakes, and help us to show our sorrow by living better in the days to come.

Help us like John constantly to speak the truth.
> Keep us from twisting the truth to conceal our own faults;
> Keep us from evading the truth we do not wish to see;

Keep us from silencing the truth, because we are more
afraid to offend men than we are to disobey you;
Save us from speaking or from acting a lie,
and save us from false words and from cowardly
silence.

Help us like John boldly to rebuke vice.
Keep us from being censorious or arrogant, self-
righteous or fault-finding;
But help us never to be silent
in the presence of injustice or impurity;
Grant that we may never see another drifting or rush-
ing to disaster without speaking the word of warning
we ought to speak in love.

Help us like John patiently to suffer for the truth.
Grant that we may set allegiance to the truth above all
worldly success;
Grant that we may be ready to face loneliness and un-
popularity for the sake of the truth;
Grant that we may follow the truth wherever it leads,
that we may obey the truth whatever it demands, that
we may speak the truth whatever it costs.

So grant that living the truth we may be the true servants of
you who are the God of truth; through Jesus Christ our
Lord. Amen.

Saint John Baptist's Day is 24th June.

Saint Peter's Day

*O Almighty God, who by thy Son Jesus Christ, didst give
to thy Apostle Saint Peter many excellent gifts, and commandest him earnestly to feed thy flock: Make, we beseech
thee, all Bishops and Pastors diligently to preach thy holy
Word, and the people obediently to follow the same, that
they may receive the crown of everlasting glory; through
Jesus Christ our Lord. Amen.*

Lesson: Acts 12.1-11 *Gospel:* Matthew 16.13-19

O God, our Father, through Jesus Christ you called Peter to
care for the flock of your Church. Bless all those who are
pastors and preachers and leaders for your people.

Help them to be,
     Diligent in their study and their preparation;
     Earnest in their prayer and their devotion;
     Faithful and loving in their visitation;
     Sincere and honest in their preaching.
Help them to be,
     Wise in administration;
     Loving and forgiving in their dealings with others,
       especially with those who are difficult;
     Honest in their thinking so that other thinkers may
     respect them;
     Clear in their speaking so that simple folk may hear
     them gladly.

Bless all the members of your Church.
Grant that,
> They may come to Church with expectation;
> They may worship in truth and sincerity;
> They may listen with humility.
> Give them minds which are eager to learn,
> and memories that are retentive to remember,
> And grant that they may go out into the world
>> To practise what they have heard,
>> And to live what they have learned.

And so grant that pastors and people may be united in love for each other, in service of men, and in witness for you; through Jesus Christ our Lord. Amen.

Saint Peter's Day is 29th June.

Saint James the Apostle

Grant, O merciful God, that as thine holy Apostle Saint James, leaving his father and all that he had, without delay was obedient unto the calling of thy Son Jesus Christ, and followed him; so we, forsaking all worldly and carnal affections, may be evermore ready to follow thy holy commandments; through Jesus Christ our Lord. Amen.

Lesson: Acts 11.27-12.3   *Gospel:* Matthew 20.20-28

Let us remember how James with John left everything to follow Jesus (Mark 1.19, 20).

O Lord, Jesus Christ, help us as James did to set loyalty to you above all earthly things. Grant that no matter what the cost we may do what you order and go where you send.

Help us to set any task to which you call us above any earthly career. Help us to remember that money and worldly success can cost too much, and help us to set obedience to you above the claims of any earthly person or thing; and grant that our love of you may surpass even the dearest and the closest human tie.

Let us remember how James with John was with Jesus at the raising of Jairus' daughter, on the Mount, in the Garden (Mark 5.37; 9.2; 14.33).

O Lord Jesus, make us such that we will be fit to be your closest friends. Make us such that we may ever see your vision and share your work, and enter into your ordeal. Make us such that you will be able to use us as voices to speak for you and hands to serve you.

Let us remember how James with John asked for the high-est place (Mark 10.35-45).

O Lord Jesus, help us with James and John never to doubt that you will come into your kingdom and that you will one day give your own reward to those who are your faithful servants, but help us like them also to learn that true greatness lies in service, and that he who would be first must be the servant of all.

Let us remember how James died a martyr for his Lord (Acts 12.2).

O Lord Jesus, give us the loyalty which will make us ready to do and to endure all things for you. Make us faithful all our days, down even to the gates of death, that in the end we may receive the crown of life.

All this we ask for your love's sake. Amen.

Saint James the Apostle's Day is 25th July.

Saint Bartholomew the Apostle

O Almighty and everlasting God, who didst give to thine Apostle Bartholomew grace truly to believe and to preach thy Word: Grant, we beseech thee, unto thy Church, to love that Word which he believed, and both to preach and receive the same; through Jesus Christ our Lord. Amen.

Lesson: Acts 5. 12-16   *Gospel:* Luke 22. 24-30

O God, our Father, you have always been speaking to men and to nations, and you are still speaking to us.

Give us grace to listen to your word.

> Grant that we may not be so busy with the world's affairs that we have no time to listen to your voice. Grant that the voice of our own desires may not be speaking so insistently that we become deaf to your word.

Give us grace to receive your word.

> Grant that we may never reject your word because it speaks to us the truth which we do not want to hear. Grant that we may never shut our ears to your word because it calls us to a way which we do not want to take.

Give us grace to believe your word.

> Grant to us to believe that your commands are meant for us and that your promises are true for us. Grant to us to believe that you will never make a demand from us which you will not help us to perform, and that you will never make a promise that you will not fulfil.

Give us grace to love your word.

Grant that we may ever turn to your word to find light for our minds, guidance for our footsteps, and comfort for our hearts.

Give us grace to preach your word.

Grant that we may be eager to share with others that which we have learned from you, and that we may be able to lead others to love you because we love you ourselves.

Give us grace to live your word.

Grant that what we hear with our ears, we may understand with our minds, and receive into our hearts, and live out in our lives.

This we ask through Jesus Christ our Lord. Amen.

Saint Bartholomew's Day is 24th August.

Saint Matthew the Apostle

O Almighty God, who by thy blessed Son didst call Matthew from the receipt of custom to be an Apostle and Evangelist: Grant us grace to forsake all covetous desires, and inordinate love of riches, and to follow the same thy Son Jesus Christ, who liveth and reigneth with thee and the Holy Ghost, one God, world without end. Amen.

Epistle: II Corinthians 4.1-6   *Gospel:* Matthew 9.9-13

O God, our Father, we know that we cannot forget the world because we have to live in it. We know that we dare not disregard the world, because it is your world, and the work of the world has to go on. We cannot entirely neglect money and material things because we have to earn a living for ourselves and for those whom we love. But at the same time help us to see things in their proper proportion and to keep things in their proper place.

> Grant that we may never be so immersed in the things of time that we forget the things of eternity.

> Grant that we may never set material profit and gain above the claims of honesty and honour.

> Grant that we may never be so concerned with getting that we forget about giving.

> Grant that we may never be so concentrated upon our own concerns that we forget the appeal of those in need.

Deliver us from all covetousness, and from the desire to possess what we have not got. Give us grace always to make the best of what we have, and give us the gift of contentment with our lot.

Give us in our lives the right and the true ambition, the ambition to find our greatness in serving others, and the ambition to put into life more than we take out.

So save us from all selfishness, and put into our lives the spirit of him who, though he was rich, yet for our sakes became poor, and who loved us and gave himself for us.
This we ask for your love's sake. Amen.

Saint Matthew's Day is 21*st September.*

Saint Michael and all Angels

O Everlasting God, who hast ordained and constituted the services of Angels and men in a wonderful order: Mercifully grant, that as thy holy Angels alway do thee service in heaven, so by thy appointment they may succour and defend us on earth; through Jesus Christ our Lord. Amen.

Lesson: Revelation 12.7-12   *Gospel:* Matthew 18.1-10

O God, our Father, we know that your Angels go willingly and obediently on any task to which you send them. In your mercy send them to us

> For the enlightenment of our minds in knowledge;
> For the guidance of our footsteps in wisdom;
> For our help in every time of difficulty and danger;
> For our defence in every hour of temptation.

Grant that they may be to us

> The messengers,
>   who tell us of your will;
> The guides,
>   who show us where we ought to go;
> The helpers,
>   who aid us
>   when we are upon an engagement very difficult;
> The protectors,
>   who defend us against the assaults of the Evil One.

Make us even upon earth to feel around us and about us the powers of heaven, so that we may know that there is always with us a power which is not our power, to help us to overcome evil and to do the right, and so to live victoriously; through Jesus Christ our Lord. Amen.

The day of Saint Michael and all Angels is 29th September.

Saint Luke the Evangelist

Almighty God, who calledst Luke the Physician, whose praise is in the Gospel, to be an Evangelist, and Physician of the soul: May it please thee, that, by the wholesome medicines of the doctrine delivered by him, all the diseases of our souls may be healed; through the merits of thy Son Jesus Christ our Lord. Amen.

Epistle: II Timothy 4.5-15   *Gospel:* Luke 10.1-7a

O God, our Father, we remember today that you called Luke the beloved doctor to be the writer of a Gospel and a missionary of the Kingdom. Give to us this day healing of body, mind and spirit.

Give us health of body.

Make us fit to do our work and to earn a living for ourselves and for those we love. Rid us of such habits and self-indulgences as would injure our bodies, and which would make us less fit to serve you and to serve our fellow men. And help us always to remember that our bodies are meant to be the temple and the dwelling-place of your Holy Spirit, and that it is our duty to offer them as a living sacrifice to you.

Give us health of mind.

Keep our thoughts from dwelling on evil, soiled or forbidden things. Give us honesty, sincerity, and openness of mind, that we may recognize, understand and obey the truth. Give us peace of mind that we may be saved from the tension and from the strain, from the worry and from the anxiety, which make life collapse and break down. Give us a healthy mind in a healthy body.

Give us health of spirit.

Protect us from the temptations which would injure our purity and defend us from the sins which are always ready to fascinate and to seduce us. So cleanse us that we may be pure in heart and so see you; and so help us to wait on you that our strength may be daily renewed.

So grant that, healed and purified, strengthened and renewed, in body, mind and spirit, we may serve you and serve our fellow men in gladness, in peace, and in power; through Jesus Christ our Lord. Amen.

Saint Luke the Evangelist's Day is 18*th October.*

Saint Simon and Saint Jude, Apostles

O Almighty God, who hast built thy Church upon the foundation of the Apostles and Prophets, Jesus Christ himself being the head corner-stone: Grant us so to be joined together in unity of spirit by their doctrine, that we may be made an holy temple acceptable unto thee; through Jesus Christ our Lord. Amen.

Epistle: Jude 1-8   *Gospel:* John 15.17-27

O God, our Father, we thank you for those on whom your Church is founded and built:

> For the apostles,
>> who lived and who died,
>>> to bring the gospel to a world which had never known it;
>
> For the prophets,
>> who fearlessly proclaimed your truth,
>> and who without fear and without favour
>>> spoke to men what you had spoken to them.

Above all we thank you for Jesus Christ, the foundation and the head corner-stone, on whom the Church is built and by whom the Church is sustained.

Grant unto us in our day and generation that true unity of spirit which will make us one.

Help us at all times,
>   To hold one faith;
>   To serve one Lord;
>   To live in one love;
>   To seek one goal.

To that end us keep us
>   From the disharmony which divides;
>   From the disunity which disturbs the peace;
>   From the disputing which separates those who should be one.

Grant that
>   We may never love systems
>   more than we love Jesus Christ;
>   We may never love doctrines
>   more than we love men;
>   We may never make creeds
>   a barrier to divide rather than a bond to unite.

So grant that built on one common foundation, holding one common faith, loving one common Lord, your Church may be a fit dwelling for your Holy Spirit; through Jesus Christ our Lord. Amen.

St Simon and St Jude's Day is 28th October.

All Saints' Day

O Almighty God, who hast knit together thine elect in one communion and fellowship, in the mystical body of thy Son Christ our Lord: Grant us grace so to follow thy blessed Saints in all virtues and godly living, that we may come to those unspeakable joys, which thou hast prepared for them that unfeignedly love thee; through Jesus Christ our Lord. Amen.

Lesson: Revelation 7.2-12   *Gospel:* Matthew 5.1-12

Eternal God, make us this day to remember the unseen cloud of witnesses who compass us about:

> Those who in every age and generation
>> witnessed to their faith in life and in death;
> Those who by their courage and their sacrifice
>> won for us the freedom and the liberty we enjoy;
> Those who served their fellow men
>> at the cost of pain, of persecution and of death;
> Those for whom all the trumpets sounded
>> as they passed over to the other side;
> Those whom we have loved and who have gone to be with you,
>> and whose names are written on our hearts.

Help us to walk worthily of those in whose unseen presence life is lived. Help us to have in our lives

> Their courage in danger;
> Their stedfastness in trial;
> Their perseverance in difficulty;

Their loyalty when loyalty is costly;
Their love which nothing can change;
Their joy which nothing can take away.

So grant to us in your good time to share with them the blessedness of your nearer presence, that we also may come to that life,

Where all the questions are answered;
Where all the tears are wiped away;
Where we shall meet again, never to be separated from
them, those whom we have loved and lost awhile;
Where we shall be for ever with our Lord.

So grant to us in this life never to forget those who have gone before, so that in the life to come we may share their blessedness; through Jesus Christ our Lord. Amen.

All Saints' Day is 1st November.

INDEX